Children
and
Nonviolence

Bob and Janet Aldridge

Hope Publishing House
Pasadena

D1206359

Children and Nonviolence. ©1987 by Bob and Janet
Aldridge. All rights reserved. For information address
Hope Publishing House, P.O. Box 60008, Pasadena, CA 91106.
Printed in the United States of America.

First Edition

Manuscript Editor: Faith Annette Sand
Cover Design: Michael McClary/The Workshop

Library of Congress Cataloging-in Publication Data

Aldridge, Bob, 1926-
    Children and nonviolence.

    1.   Child rearing–Religious aspects–Christianity.
2. Nonviolence–Religious aspects–Christianity. 3. Child
psychology.
I. Aldridge, Janet, 1928-   . II. Title.
HQ769.3.A44 1986 649'.1 87-4126

ISBN 0-932727-18-2
ISBN 0-932727-17-4 (pbk.)

To Cres, Janie, Jim, Dan, Kathy, Teri, Mary, Diane, Nancy and Mark who helped us grow as parents.

Table of Contents

Introduction

Marriage is that relation
between man and woman
in which the independence is equal,
the dependence mutual,
and the obligations reciprocal.
— *Louis Kaufman Anspacher*
Boston Address (12/30/34)

We began our life together on August 17, 1947. During the intervening years we have had fun and misery, raised ten children, made mistakes and achieved successes, redirected our values several times, worked for reform in the church, and launched a campaign to stop nuclear genocide. We have been advocates of nonviolence while still retaining our conviction that the family has the most influence on society.

Janet was born a Catholic and raised on a farm near the little town of Tyndall, South Dakota. She attended the local schools until halfway through her senior high school year when, in early 1946, she moved to California to take a receptionist job in an office where her brother worked, finishing up her last year at Watsonville High School.

Bob was born a Protestant, raised in and around Watsonville, California and graduated from Watsonville High School in 1943. He then went into the army to see combat in the Philippines during World War II. We met shortly after Bob's discharge in 1946 when he enrolled in California State Polytechnic University at San Luis Obispo to study aeronautical engineering.

In early 1947 we became engaged and were married in August. A 17-foot trailer house on the Cal Poly campus became our home and soon we developed a close community with other student couples and their children, sharing everything from coin-op washing machines and a pay telephone booth to community showers and toilets. During this time Bob started taking instructions to become a Catholic.

While we were in the trailer house our first child was born. Creston was a robust little rascal who injected great joy into our marriage. Shortly thereafter he and Bob were both baptized into the Catholic church which began what we now call the dogmatic Catholic phase of our marriage.

By December 1948 Bob had earned a two-year technical degree in aeronautics and his aviation mechanic licenses. As we were anxious to get settled and have an income, we left Cal Poly. These were the pre-Korean War recession years when jobs were hard to find and, rather than hiring, the big aircraft companies were laying workers off. After several months of futile search Bob settled for a job with the California State Forestry and we made a down payment on our first home in Watsonville. During the six forestry years Janie, Jim and Danny were born. Most of our neighbors were young couples with small children and we had a lot in common.

In 1955 Bob left the Forestry and obtained a job driving a butane truck. Kathy was born shortly after Bob started this job and Teri came along just before he left, bringing our children to six.

In 1956 Lockheed Corporation started moving its missile and space operations to Sunnyvale which is at the southern end of San Francisco Bay. Bob looked into employment possibilities and found them good. We were then faced with the pros and cons of moving. It was a difficult decision because we owned our own home, had adequate time for recreation and were happy among good friends. Moving would mean giving up a home we liked for something unknown, living in a congested area, making new friends and changing schools for Cres and Janie. But it would give Bob a chance to get back into aeronautical engineering.

We finally decided to move but made a promise to God that if we made lots of money we would use it to raise our children to be good citizens and good Christians. That covenant didn't seem too significant at the time but now we see that it was our first overt commitment to follow God's will as we understood it.

Our Lockheed paychecks started in May 1957. Bob also started evening courses to finish his bachelor of science degree. But it was not easy to sell the house in Watsonville and it was difficult to find a suitable new one. Bob had to board during the week in San Jose and Janet was again saddled with 24-hour responsibility for the children. This trial, thankfully, only lasted six months and just before Christmas we were able to move into our present home in Santa Clara.

Advancement was good at Lockheed; Bob received his degree in 1962 and Mary, Diane, Nancy and Mark were born to complete our family of ten children. The future looked bright. Many seemingly small bits and pieces fell into place to help us. Regular overtime the first few years cleared our debts and paid off the second mortgage on our new home. When Bob had taken all the courses he could at night, Lockheed started an evening engineering shift which allowed him to attend daytime classes. When all his courses were completed, the evening shift just happened to be discontinued. All coincidences? Maybe. But we felt there was a guiding force orchestrating our lives.

Until we moved to Santa Clara we had been traditional Catholics, authoritarian parents and unquestioning citizens. Shortly after settling into our new home we were invited to join a Christian Family Movement (CFM) group and were impressed that the people who approached us went out of their way to welcome us to the community. Their warmth, more than anything, made us attentive to the CFM meetings that followed.

CFM is aimed at helping married couples see the Christian dimension of family life and the importance of the family in society. The principles of Observe, Judge and Act are used with a heavy emphasis on the action. During the first year the group focused on the family and its immediate neighborhood environment. Later the observations, judgments and actions branched out to the social, political and economic sectors of society. With this exposure to a wide range of ideas our own rigid ways began to flex.

In 1963 we were introduced to the Cursillo (Cursillo de Christiandad), which is a little course in Christianity started in Spain that eventually migrated around the world to the United States. The course consists of a three-day experience of intensive Christian community.

Each day has a theme. The first day is Piety—to facilitate our looking inside ourselves and dispelling false notions to arrive at a wholesome concept of spirituality. Next comes Study—to become informed about what to study and when. The final day focuses on Action and ends with a call to commitment which fits the various individuals' circumstances and motivations. For us the Piety-Study-Action of the Cursillo seemed to compliment the Observe-Judge-Act of CFM. Both were aimed at informed activity and had a lasting effect on us.

All of this spiritual reevaluation and energizing was accomplished in the spirit of Vatican Ecumenical Council II during which Pope John XXIII opened a "window" of the Catholic church to let in some fresh air. In similar fashion we opened a window to our beliefs and that caused some changes. By 1968 we were beginning to question many traditional practices in our efforts to move closer to the basic truths taught by Jesus. In so doing we became more open to the truths God had revealed to other people through other traditions and cultures.

It was inevitable that we perceived a new dimension to the war that was then being fought in Indochina and soon began acting on these insights to oppose that conflict. We also started questioning the designing of weapons as the source of our own bread and butter. As our awareness increased, we recognized sinister shifts in U.S. nuclear strategy. Our involvement with those who were putting their lives on the line for peace and justice gave us the courage to disengage ourselves from weapons production early in 1973.

Questions naturally followed. We believed we were acting according to conscience, but there seemed to be a contradiction. Why did God smooth the way toward success, or so it seemed, and then ask us to give it all up? By human standards it didn't make sense, but there must have been a reason. At this juncture all we could do was follow what signs we could see. Again we made a promise to God: we would do our best to respond to the circumstances placed in our path. Little did we foresee what that would lead to.

Since ending our complicity with the military-industrial complex we have tried to help others understand what building nuclear weapons and implementing our current military programs means for the future. Our livelihood now comes from Bob's writing and lecturing on that subject and from Janet's working with minority children in public schools. This has led to traveling and meeting many people of different faiths and maturing in the process.

Looking back at some of our failures in family raising we now realize that we tried to do what seemed right at the time, but our perceptions of right did not remain static. They have changed as we have changed. What seems most important to us now is to learn from our failures as well as successes; which means constantly reassessing values and altering our behavior patterns. Although this is not easy, without that ability to change there is no growth as a person, as a spouse or as a parent. Failure to change when necessary is not merely standing still, it is moving backward relative to our environment. The world goes on and leaves us in the past.

To grow with society we must change at the same rate. To be a leader in society requires changing at a faster rate; assuming our society is moving in a direction which will enhance life for its members without being detrimental to our global neighbors. If society is going astray and we move with it, we lose our identity in the formless mass of nonthinkers who unwittingly drift toward extinction. That is what we see happening to so many today where greed and self-interests are aggravating the nuclear menace and resources are diminished faster than they can be renewed.

The way to be a leader in a drifting society is to change in a different direction—a corrective direction. This puts one at odds with public acceptance and elicits persecution for being different or for appearing presumptuous in deciding that we are right and the masses are wrong. At this point we need to search our conscience and seek divine guidance.

It may seem like a contradiction to admit that we do not have all the answers and are willing to change as new knowledge presents itself, and yet presume to have better insight than many in society. Yet when one diligently strives for the truth, one must follow that perceived truth wherever it may lead—hanging onto it regardless of the consequences. The arms race and global extinction, to say nothing of the misery and deaths caused by our misplaced priorities, are so far from any true spiritual teaching that they cannot be confused with such. As one makes an attempt to discover the truth, God helps in the focusing process. Those who try to recognize truth do not self-righteously look upon themselves as depositaries of all wisdom. Rather, by putting themselves at God's disposal to accomplish God's work, they recognize that all truth and knowledge comes from God.

One overarching conviction has grown in our thinking: the dollar priority in America—or the tendency to measure everything by the economic yardstick—has subverted our more important values. Against this backdrop, marriage has degenerated to trial and error at best and sexual license at worst. As the chance for wholesome family living diminishes, children are conditioned with the same traits that are moving humanity toward extinction. As marriage and family life continue to fail because of false values, a weakening society tends to blame marriage for its ills. Instead of trying to raise marriage and family life to their full potential, these institutions are frequently rejected as people unsuccessfully seek substitutes; which often merely aggravates the problem.

Marriage and family are still the basic building blocks of society and if these blocks are soft and crumbly, society is unstable. Only when society and community are in equilibrium is society well, and only when marriage and family are founded on unselfish love can community happen. The family as a biological entity is not enough. A loving family community is needed to form a healthy society.

The family is an integral part of all communities, or should be. We do not mean the so-called nuclear family which forms a tight clique in a competitive society. What we envision as family is a small and basic community which is in harmony with other families and the larger community. There are many types of communities—intentional, religious, for singles, for married couples with children and more. Many have sprung up as experiments in response to the failure of the family. In our experience we have found the primary family community to be vital. No other forms of community possess the critical and unique potential of the family community for nurturing their citizens for a just and peaceful society.

Today when half of our families are single-parent homes, the love between parent and children is extremely critical for balancing the overtaxing energy demands on the single parent. In spite of the stress placed on single parents, many of our friends handling such roles are doing magnificent jobs raising children—often better than some dual-parent families we know. We are convinced that these nonviolent principles are equally valid for both situations. Since most of the single-parent families stem from divorce or separation, it is our hope that we may stimulate a better understanding of marriage so that many split ups will not occur in the first place.

This book is based on our lives. In it we share our experiences, successes and mistakes so that others may benefit from our practical applications of theories developed in four decades of learning and attempting to maintain an atmosphere of love and belonging between ourselves and with our children.

Because our family is large it may be helpful to furnish the following timetable:

Bob and Janet	Married Aug 17, 1947
Creston (Cres)	Born May 13, 1948
Jane (Janie)	Born Oct 23, 1949
James (Jim)	Born Mar 23, 1952
Daniel (Dan or Danny)	Born Oct 19, 1953
Kathleen (Kathy)	Born May 16, 1955
Teri	Born Jan 23, 1957
Mary	Born Feb 11, 1959
Diane	Born Sep 14, 1964
Nancy	Born Nov 13, 1966
Mark	Born Dec 9, 1969

A word about the manner in which we use viewpoint and gender in this book. Mostly we will be writing in the first person plural but occasionally we will refer to one or the other of us in the third person singular, usually by name. Also, when referring to a choice of either masculine or feminine as a third person singular pronoun, we will use the plural "they" or "their." This is not precise English but is less awkward than using the term "he or she" and more desireable than using only one gender to signify both.

We wish to express our deepest thanks to all those people who have helped us and encouraged us to write this book; and particularly Jim and Kathy McGinnis and Roxanne Province who spent much time reviewing the draft manuscript, giving us important criticism, suggestions and encouragement. Also thanks to our children who have read early drafts and added their comments.

Bob and Janet Aldridge
Santa Clara, California

The root of the kingdom
is in the state.
The root of the state.
is in the family.

—Mencius
372-289 B.C.
The Chinese Classics, Vol. II

1

Marriage as the Wellspring of Nonviolence

Seldom, or perhaps never, does a marriage develop into an individual relationship smoothly and without crisis; there is no coming to consciousness without pain.

—*Carl Gustav Jung*
Contribution to Analytical
Psychology.

When young Lisa first visited our home she was in kindergarten. Half black and half Chicana, she had already experienced a hectic five years of life. Children adjust to such circumstances but not in the way which promotes a healthy society. Her father's alcohol problem kept him chronically unemployed and, more often than not, away from home. Her mother was always sick and left the child rearing to the older children who had their own preoccupation with street gangs.

We met Lisa and her younger sister through a CFM activity and our home soon became her refuge. She looked forward to weekends with us or a camping trip into the mountains. Her vision was poor and we were continually arranging for eye examinations and glasses. Her own parents just didn't seem to have time for such attention. She brought lice infestations when she arrived and we usually had to diplomatically remove our children's belongings from her bag before she left—toys and other articles which happened to be inadvertently packed.

Lisa was in grade school when her mother died. She was too distraught to attend the funeral. Her aunt took charge and moved the family to New York. Lisa occasionally contacted us, mostly when she needed help. From what we can determine she dropped out of school to become a bar dancer and prostitute. Her infrequent communication was heartbreaking.

Our encounter with Lisa indelibly impressed upon us how vital a harmonious marriage is in fostering nonviolent attitudes in youngsters. It is from this base that healthy values spring. Children and family were meant to start with two people loving each other in a more profound way than they love friends or relatives—a love which includes not only physical, emotional and psychological intimacy but also a deep spiritual bond to one another and to God.

Marriage is first of all that tremendous love and dedication to each other—a striving to place the marriage partner's happiness as top priority rather than being selfish. Some degree of accomplishment of this feat is the secret of a successful marriage. Most divorces are caused by the inability of one or both spouses to overcome what Karl Menninger calls selfism—that pseudo religion of ego inflation and self-worship. In a society where our environment—the whole gamut from formal education to television commercials—is geared toward instant gratification, it is difficult to pause long enough to consider others. Yet feeling and concern for each other is necessary for a marriage to endure. Willpower and determination play a very significant role in overcoming self-interests.

This sounds like work and maybe that is why some people just give up. But it comes right down to values. When we want something badly enough we are willing to work for it. Conversely, the harder we work for something, the more valuable it becomes. So it is with marriage. Emphasis should not be on the 50 percent of marriages that end in divorce, but rather should pay particular attention to the other half that stay together. Those are the couples who have gone through trials and crises like everyone else, but they have found some way to overcome those difficulties.

For some couples, their vocation to each other is the extent of their marriage and that is good if that is what they want. But marriage has even greater dimensions—the raising of children. Without tremendous love and dedication the bringing up of children can be catastrophic. Meeting the physical, psychological and spiritual needs of children is a huge responsibility, the dimensions of which are virtually impossible to comprehend. Even after four decades of raising our ten children we are still awed at the influence parents possess.

All children have a right to a happy family life with a loved and loving father and mother. Even though thousands of youngsters are not allowed that right does not make them less deserving of it. Denial of this basic right is a smudge on our success as human beings and on our society as a whole. We might not be able to do much about the death of a parent, but we could greatly reduce the number of broken homes, unwanted children, as well as acts of child abuse. Children need intimate day-to-day relationships with parents and the security fostered by a visible love between parents.

Holding the marriage relationship in high esteem goes a long way in fostering this healthy family atmosphere. Marriage needs to be recognized as sacred. The wedding ceremony and the vows, the living together and the raising of children are the visible aspects of this sacrament. Beneath the surface of human perception is a deep and dynamic activity which even the marriage partners cannot fully understand, but to which they are called to respond. Marriage is a call to delve into this mystery and to share the discoveries found with one another so that the spirituality of the marriage can be better perceived by all.

Marriage is meant to be permanent, no matter how unstable other things around us may be. We promised that permanency to each other "until death do us part" and meant that vow. Even though it seems most people want to mean it when they vow nonending loyalty to each other, divorce statistics indicate that permanency does not endure in half the marriages undertaken. Against this statistical backdrop it is hard to maintain a healthy perception of the sacredness of marriage.

We do not have a complete answer to the problems

facing marriage today but we can share our story and try to analyze the forces which affected us. Having been married since 1947 sets some sort of a record by today's standards although we are still not beyond the point where divorces occur. But there are a few recognizable ingredients which we believe helped our love to endure.

Taking these in chronological order, probably the first boon to our lasting power was our attitude toward marriage during our premarital years. Neither of us came from a broken home; a definite advantage in helping us believe in the sacredness and permanence of marriage. After all, when people tend to see themselves as less capable than their parents, who may be divorced, and who are raised knowing that half the marriages consummated will eventually fail, it is harder to enter into marriage without feeling fatalistic. Of course such statistical predetermination is a false concept for we make of our life what we allow ourselves to make of it. By mustering self-confidence and using free will to maintain a personality sensitive to others, we can make our marriages into joyful encounters, despite the odds. By so doing we in turn make it easier for our children to experience this same happiness.

Janet believes that because her parents, relatives and friends all had enduring marriages, this influenced her attitude toward permanency. One of the greatest impressions her mother and dad made on her was their complete trust in each other. Neither doubted the other and they allowed each other the freedom to manifest their own personality.

One thing that greatly helped Bob during his adolescent years was having frequent discussions with his dad. The conversation once got onto the subject of purity. Bob still remembers his dad telling him: "If you save yourself for your wedding night, it will be the most beautiful night in your life." Such advice might seem archaic by today's standards, but some old fashioned ideas have a lot of merit. That remark helped him through many temptations—especially when he was in the army where morals were low, even among married men. Dad probably never realized what a lasting impact those words had but they cut through the notion that sex is cheap and brought a sense of values into focus.

Such a wholesome outlook toward marriage is hard for today's young people when radios, television, newspapers, books, movies and signboards all exploit the sensationalism of sex. Advice columnists use terms like "sex partners" as a worldly substitute for husband and wife. Even the most notable authors usually have their characters jumping into bed as soon as they decide they are in love, as if that realization justifies such behavior. When continuously bombarded with this type of propaganda—frequently attempting to sell some commodity—it is not surprising that young people see casual sex as the expected behavior when dating. Of course natural desires reinforce rationalization about sexual freedom. This self-fulfilling syndrome has nothing to do with genuine sexuality and certainly does not enhance the dignity of marriage.

Such overemphasis on sex often motivates couples to enter into marriage without developing a love that is more than skin deep. Physical attractiveness is probably the least important attribute to consider when picking a lifelong partner. Less visible personality traits (like patience, generosity, respect and understanding) are much more vital and longer lasting.

This leads to a frequent delusion involved when young couples live together prior to marriage, frequently to determine compatibility. Such a "try before you buy" test does not necessarily engender caring and respect or any serious dedication to each other. The results are usually disappointing when the interest in compatibility centers on personal concerns. On the other hand, when selfless love predominates, and interpersonal depth is the goal, the importance of compatibility diminishes. Such deeply-rooted love can be developed without living together, but it does require time and patience. For that reason hasty marriages often are problematic. Practicing personal chastity, patience and mutual respect is undoubtedly the most profound preparation for marriage. These mold selfless attitudes and interpersonal depths which lead to a successful marriage and a wholesome family atmosphere.

Some couples live together without going through a

public marriage ceremony because they have rejected the traditional institution of marriage. Having seen the hypocrisy of friends and relatives vowing to be true unto death and then parting in a few years, these couples choose to forgo the formalities. Many are sincere and do make private vows, others merely choose to live together temporarily. Whatever the arrangement, it does not appear that these alternative relationships have reduced the number of psychologically upset children with poor moral values.

The public wedding ceremony is important because it does much more than provide the civil legality to a conjugal relationship. Marriage has a public nature because it is an important building block of society. Thus the wedding promises are more than private and spiritual. As they have a public nature, it is fitting that they should be broadcast. The community also deserves the opportunity to pray and rejoice with the couple as they embark on their vocation. Every marriage interacts with society which helps direct it. The right direction starts with the public proclamation.

Something that seems to have helped our love endure is that we have had periodic changes which help to keep romance and challenge alive. Such changes might be necessary to a successful marriage. Psychologists tell us that people change in approximate seven year cycles. Just as physically every seven years the human body completely changes substance, so in a similar manner we go through a mental change every six to eight years which often results in a growing dissatisfaction with our job, our living location, and other aspects of our life. If we do not have a change of environment to freshen things up a bit, our outlook on life can sour. This phenomenon seems to be an actual functioning of our minds and bodies, not just a conditioning of the throw-away culture which fosters a yearning for more and better things.

If this theory is true, how can we reconcile it with the idea of permanence in marriage? Here are two people who promise themselves to each other for life, yet seven years later they are to a large extent two different people. The solution to this dilemma derives from understanding that there is more to our being than just mind and body.

Our commitment in marriage has far more depth and mystery attached to it than a commitment to a job or a particular locality. The marriage bond far transcends emotions; whereas attachment to profession or neighborhood is largely emotional, varying from nostalgia to fear for financial security. If marriage is of higher priority, lesser commitments must give way when they conflict.

First take a hypothetical case which could apply to many of our friends and acquaintances who are divorced. Two people start off in marriage full of love and enthusiasm. They struggle together to obtain a house and raise children. More often than not the husband, and frequently the wife, are also struggling to establish themselves in their chosen occupation. There are times of joy, times of sorrow and times of conflict, but they hang in there together. Not only is this period challenging and romantic, but the mutual struggle also strengthens the bond between husband and wife.

A decade or two passes and the situation changes. The two principals are chemically different than when they married each other years before. That aspect probably is not as important as the psychological and philosophical changes which have occurred. If both husband and wife have moved in the same direction then they are probably still happy together, but if those changes have been frustrated in one or both, then divorce is imminent if it has not already happened.

Frustration of emotional growth can be recognized by boredom and being tired of the rat race. The wife may be unhappy with the housework routine or the increasing job demands on her husband's time which keep him away from the family. These are danger signals. Should corrective action be put off for fear of financial insecurity, or a feeling that there is too much invested in the job to leave it, or an attachment to the house, or many other seemingly valid reasons, then the relationship between husband and wife will often deteriorate. As frustration increases, it tends to be vented on those who are closest and the magnitude of some frustrations can wreck a marriage. For marriages to survive, they need safety valves. Changing the situation is simply a matter of priorities, although it is often delayed until too late.

In our own experience we were not so smart that we did everything right, but we were fortunate enough to blunder into making some decisions which were right for us (faith and prayer undoubtedly helped). Our experience may be helpful to others.

Our first crisis surfaced some five years into our marriage. Bob was working for the State Forestry and spending five days a week away from home leaving Janet to feel the crunch of having sole responsibility for the children. After several years of trying to work out alternatives Bob finally left that occupation and took a temporary truck driving job. Our family was not only reunited every evening but, the job being a local delivery route, we also had lunch together every day. The new experience of togetherness stimulated our marriage. It was an opportunity to fall in love all over again. In the process we also discovered that time at home is a sacred priority. In this case we worked together, matured in the same direction, and the result of change was good.

Our second crisis was more minor and we were able to resolve it before it gained significant proportions. After Bob had worked at Lockheed for seven or eight years he found his tasks there to be routine and unchallenging. A transfer to another department and another field of work opened new horizons. That solved the immediate problem and change revitalized his personality. Concurrently, we were working and changing together in the spiritual dimension—from the Christian Family and the Cursillo movements, to adult education in the parish, to lay groups seeking reform within the church, to liturgical communities. All of these, undertaken in the spirit of the Second Vatican Ecumenical Council, had a profound effect on our personalities.

A major crisis swelled during the 1970s when Bob hit a moral snag regarding the nuclear missile design work he was doing. We worked it out together and moved in the same direction, although it involved a big revision in lifestyle. Work habits and family roles also changed and that produced subsequent minor crises—aftershocks, if you will. Our solution led to new challenges and a surge of romance in our lives. Had Janet insisted that Bob continue in the weapons industry because of financial responsibility to the family, or had Bob refused to give up status and seniority, it is hard to predict what may have happened. That is why we are convinced it is important to change together, although that does not mean conforming to one or the other. Each partner needs to freely exercise their unique talents or they will stagnate and cause a new crisis.

Since Bob left war work we have met others still in the industry who would like to quit building weapons but who are in the sad situation where the spouse will not tolerate the accompanying change in living habits. There are also other cases where one spouse wants the other to quit war work, but they refuse. These are much more complex situations than weighing a job against marriage, for it puts a person in the cross fire between conscience and marriage. At such a juncture one would be well advised to concentrate on prayerful discussion while seeking counseling with some insightful person. Experimenting with a simpler life-style and investigating how others live on less would also be helpful. Recognizing and facing up to personal fears is an important first step. Where husband and wife have grown apart, they must cautiously reevaluate their priorities if their union is to endure.

Another common situation is where couples have experienced so much change during their marriage that relief from change is needed. Possibly experimenting with a more permanent pattern of living is in order. But whatever the conditions, this periodic upheaval of dissatisfaction should be viewed as an indicator that we are ready for further growth and that we should reach for another plateau before we stagnate. It seems that God can guide us if we are responsive to seeking the direction in which God wants us to move.

One of the surest indications of getting into a psychological rut is when we start taking each other for granted. Expecting certain behavior from each other breeds resentment. In a healthy marriage we continually demonstrate love for each other by sharing tasks, bringing in a rose, expressing appreciation, leaving a note or showing affection. When we constantly look for new depths in the other's personality and rejoice together when a heretofore hidden nuance presents itself, we find ourselves on the opposite pole from taking each other for granted.

Often people attempt to pacify their unrest by buying more possessions. This false cure makes the situation worse. Those who can acquire all they desire soon become bored and more unhappy. Boredom breeds avarice and increased acquisition of goods creates anxiety over maintaining the inflated life-style. The rut deepens as attention increasingly centers on material objects. Interpersonal sensitivity withers as one becomes worldly and hard.

Repercussions from the seven-year change may be manifested in other ways. Are we unable to stand the work we are doing? Is there something about our living location that bothers us? These could also be signs that something in our life needs adjusting. If something must give, it is important that it not be the marriage because the consequences affect all the family and society.

Altering our living pattern may include a change in roles for both husband and wife. If one or both are away from the children too much, it may be necessary to rearrange schedules so that each parent can spend ample time with the family. A new division of labor often helps. Both parents may need to work part-time so that they share equally the housework and nurturing of children. However these things are worked out, the result should be what suits both parents and children. Earning more money while relegating the toddlers to day-care centers may turn out to be a foolish investment. Furthermore, the rescheduling of functions should not be done to conform to preconceived roles handed down either by tradition or the avant-garde. Outside coercion should be minimized when making family decisions. That does not mean, of course, that sound advice should be ignored.

Communication, always a criterion for happiness, is paramount when important decisions draw near. It is so vital that all impediments to honest and forthright communication should be dismantled.

To us, marriage has both a personal and public nature. As a deep experience, a feeling of closeness, a sharing of joys and sorrows, it is personal. But our marriage also affects our children and our circle of acquaintances in society. In that respect it is public and our vows, personal as they may be, are also a public statement of our contribution to society. We see the marriage ceremony as important in making that statement.

Marriage is a sacred commitment before God as well as society. We believe it is the selfless giving of ourselves to God through each other. This means that we are an avenue to divinity for our partner. Selfishness is the enemy of marriage. Personal ego is an obstacle in marriage. On the other hand, faith and prayer provide the life spirit in marriage. Our unity takes precedence over personal desires when there is conflict. In our relationship, neither one of us should oppress the other. This is the promise we make to each other. Together we share life—both the good and bad events. And in our sharing we give our lives to God.

We see marriage as a mystery and a challenge. It is looking for and discovering new mysteries in each other. It is continually falling in love with each other over and over and over again, and it is the active demonstration of that love every day of our lives.

These are our thoughts on how to keep love alive in marriage. Perhaps the most important part is being able to say "I Love You"—not in a perfunctory way, not out of long established habit, but with fresh meaning and sincerity and passion. And it's nice to get at least three hugs a day also.

2

The Family Community

A family is a place where minds come in contact with one another. If those minds love one another, the home is as beautiful as a flower garden. But if those minds get out of harmony with one another, it is like a storm that plays havoc with the garden.　　　　　　　—*The Teachings of Buddha*

Love pervades the room as we gather for the family meal tonight. Fewer of us live at home now but the feeling of mutual belonging prevails. Images flash through our minds of those absent, accompanied by a joyful feeling of gratification from their accomplishments. The older ones, on their own now, have all chosen nonexploitive careers which help others. Those still at home, disregarding some adolescent bravado, have similar plans for their lives. These nonviolent choices are the product of love. Mahatma Gandhi described nonviolence as a state of active love. We use the two terms interchangeably because, invariably, when there is conscious love there is an absence of violence. In spite of all our weaknesses and mistakes, this loving atmosphere is the only explanation of our family's contribution to society.

"Family community" is a good term to describe the primary unit of society. When a family is in community it has a good effect on family members as well as others with whom those members come in contact. This community starts with a healthy relationship between mother and father and reaches to the children with the assurance that they are wanted, loved and very precious. The binding force is a love which binds all members together.

This family spirit should not be interpreted as the haughty attitude which places family matters above those of the wider community. Rather it is a spirit that radiates outward to spread the joy and love the family is experiencing. Family jokes and traditions are part of this spirit which also serves to communicate the love and joy all members share. Communication is critical because for family members to love each other they need to know and understand one another. That means communicating to the depths of their inner feelings.

An effective stimulant to communication is to hold family meetings periodically. We have found this harder now that the children still at home are older, but still we try to have our evening meal together. Normally our talk is informal, exchanging our experiences of the day. This is facilitated when the family meal is a sit-down affair at our round, rustic, homemade table. Our time together here has become very important, and when anyone is absent they are genuinely missed. One problem is that the evening meal follows the hustle and bustle of the day. If patience is short it is better not to discuss deep subjects.

We have found a more formal type of family meeting— held perhaps weekly to plan events, solve problems and attend to other forms of family business—is vital to our family community. When these formal family councils are impractical we have fallen back on impromptu gatherings to decide specific issues as they come up. These quickie caucuses are not a good substitute for regular family meetings, however.

Family meetings were very important to us in planning Bob's escape from war work at Lockheed's missile factory. Our escape plan outlined the various tasks to be accomplished—job opportunities to investigate, people to consult, training available, etc.—with a timetable for each. We found our family councils were a major contribution toward making our decision a family decision and unifying our efforts toward life affirming activities. Such dialogue also prompted the children to see ways they could help by performing certain tasks and cutting corners on expenses.

These family meetings significantly increase mutual understanding, which is the real substance of family spirit. It works well to let the children take turns along with the parents at chairing these meetings. Our daughter Nancy prefers to start with a "compliment time" where each one tells the others something that is really appreciated about them. That usually sets the tone for good dialogue. Sometimes children balk at attending family meetings for one reason or another. We found it best not to force attendance. This, too, is part of their learning to make decisions because if anyone chooses not to attend then they must abide by the decisions reached by others. Responsible participation in decision making at all levels is a vital part of nonviolent behavior and it begins in the family.

We seek to reach decisions by consensus, which means that each person feels comfortable with the decisions reached even though they might not reflect all of their preferences. Consensus can even be used in areas such as setting limits for the children, because mom and dad also must be comfortable with what is decided. A family has much more spirit when all members feel they have a say in how family life is run, rather than having rules decreed by mother and father. Even so, heated arguments do occur and we have not completely overcome our domineering tendencies. Concensus is a more difficult practice than majority rule but it eliminates the subtle violence of imposed decisions on the outvoted minority. It also obviates the noxious practice of collusion to gain a majority.

It goes without saying that a child does need limits, which they normally struggle to stretch. Experimenting and testing is all part of growing up. It is the proper exercise of parental authority to allow such experimenting and testing as much as is safe or prudent. In the end, limits must be there and only expanded as responsibility increases. Sometimes children become disgruntled or angry for a time when they are denied something, but we have found that as they grow older they have greater respect for parents who firmly uphold just limits than for a mother or father from whom they can wheedle their way. It seems to work better, though, if decisions can be put off until the next family meeting. A time lapse seems to allow a more agreeable and harmonious decision to evolve.

Another type of family meeting which enhanced understanding among family members was introduced by Diane, and modeled after her high school values class. In one instance she had each of us draw a family crest—a heart, circle or whatever we envisioned as a good symbol. We then divided the crest into six parts and drew a picture in each section which responded to the following questions:

1. How do you make people laugh?
2. How do other people see you?
3. What is your motto in life?
4. What do you want to be remembered for?
5. What is your most offensive trait?
6. What is an accomplishment you are proud of?

Then in turn we explained these simple drawings to the others and in the process learned a lot about one another as we shared deep feelings.

There are many variations of this encounter-type family meeting. Tapping each one's ingenuity by allowing members to take turns planning and facilitating these events has yielded some wholesome and surprising experiences. It is the naive parent who thinks they fully understand their children. With every sincere interaction there is usually some heretofore unknown nuance of their personality which surfaces.

Another method of communication which has worked well in our family is our custom of writing notes. Sometimes these serve a utilitarian function, but often they are expressions of recognition and appreciation. Notes from our children which have been taped to doors, pinned on pillows and tucked into our traveling cases will say I LOVE YOU or HURRY HOME or YOU'RE A SPECIAL PERSON. When the children were smaller the letters were often fat characters, ingeniously colored or decorated with an endearing symbol. When Teri was in high school she left a typewritten note clipped to our desk lamp which read;

There are two people in this world
Who mean an awful lot to me.
Those two are my parents
And I'm proud to be
A part of them.
With Love,
Teri

At other times the notes have a more solemn tone. On several occasions, after heated discussions which were not resolved at the time, two of our daughters have left notes explaining their feelings in a loving manner. This is a good means of conflict resolution. The one writing the note had a chance to clarify their own thoughts, expressing them without interruption. The parent receiving the note could read it privately and hear the child's position under less emotional and less confrontational conditions. These notes are kept and treasured by us because they exhibit our children's love at the same time as they are asserting their own convictions. Sometimes the topic of disagreement is never brought up again, but all concerned parties know that they understand each other better.

Traditions also help to build a family spirit. Many of these are festive occasions such as get-togethers during holidays or on birthdays. Others could be called nonsense traditions such as Santa Claus and the Easter Bunny. Even when the kids grow old enough to understand that such creatures don't exist, they still have fun playing out their role in fantasy. As in many families, we play the Tooth Fairy game. Whenever a baby tooth comes out, it is taped to a piece of paper and placed under the lucky loser's pillow. Often the trouble in our house has been a very forgetful tooth fairy. So after many nights under the pillow without the legendary transformation into a shiny dime, our children have resorted to placing the tooth in a more conspicuous location where the fairy can't miss it. Taping it to the bedroom door seems to bring better results although at the next breakfast table we tend to speculate why the tooth fairy was late—possibly because of the dime shortage.

Mark was always good at playing things out in fantasy, but he also grasps reality. Once he overheard us discussing finances at the same time he lost a tooth. That night we found the tooth taped to a piece of paper on his door, but also taped to the paper were five pennies and a nickel with an accompanying note saying this donation was for the tooth fairy "because he might be broke." These little incidents personalize otherwise silly traditions with a spirit of love.

Our children, like most, have tried to stretch their limits by pointing out some lucky friend with fewer strictures. At such times we remind them that,"You are an Aldridge," and point out that in our family we do not always do as others do, but decide for ourselves what is proper. Besides giving youngsters confidence in their own good judgment, this also appeals to a sense of family values for they see themselves as part of a special unit that upholds special standards. It also teaches children that they are the sort of person that does things correctly.

At those times when the disparity in limits set by different families can be frustrating for the children, cooperative parenting can be helpful. The ideal situation allows the parents of children who chum around together to cooperate in setting uniform standards. Inconsistency is confusing to young people, for when rules are consistent they know what to expect and can thus develop confidence in their own judgment. Confidence in their perception of right and wrong is enhanced further when rules are consistent from one family to another.

With today's hodgepodge of activities it is not always possible to associate closely with the parents of all our children's friends. We have been able to do so in some areas, such as scouts. The scouting program has a lot to offer for both boys and girls if the parents actively participate and decide how the program should be run. In spite of the quasi-military environments with some emphasis on badges and medals, scouting can develop strong moral character and a concern for others. Spiritual activities are also provided for in the scouting framework. Here exists a beautiful opportunity for parents to cooperate in guiding their children in play and experimentation.

Our youngest son, Mark, preferred soccer to scouting so with him we followed the sports route. He was fortunate to have mostly good coaches who were interested in youth and emphasized the fun of playing over winning. With a little effort we were able to establish communication with Mark's closest friends on the team and were able to provide some guidance. The main thing we found lacking in this area of involvement were opportunities to help other people. Possibly with more attention we could have found ways to incorporate that more.

We received a lot of support early in our child raising years from a program in the Catholic church called the Christian Family Movement (CFM). Our particular group was not made up of parents of children who played together, but our discussions were still very helpful. We explored many aspects of family relations pertaining to children such as the pros and cons of tying their money allowance to performing chores, welcoming their friends into our home, moderating their TV viewing, guiding the use of free time, along with other nuts and bolts aspects of parenting. Most importantly, the CFM helped us experiment with various ways of making spirituality come alive in our home. There are many other organizations through which parents can exchange ideas, work out difficulties and stimulate spiritual consciousness in the family. One is the Parenting for Peace and Justice Network *(National office at 4144 Lindell Blvd, #400, St. Louis, MO 63108)*, a robust organization addressing grass roots issues encountered while raising children today.

Discipline is another area with which parents must contend but which they invariably abhor. As necessary as it is to maintain some form of discipline, there seems to be a wide range of ideas on how it should be handled. These vary from the old fashioned "spare the rod and spoil the child" theory to the unlimited freedom some modern parents allow. We subscribe to neither extreme. Interestingly, a 1982 California report, "Ounces of Prevention: Toward an Understanding of the Causes of Violence" by the California Commission on Crime control and Violence Prevention, indicates that between 84 and 97 percent of American parents use some form of physical force on their children. Yet the report points out that research findings consistently show that physical punishment, even if not obviously abusive, is not the most effective means of disciplining the child since it can produce resentment, anger, insensitivity to punishment, low frustration tolerance and lack of empathy toward others. When the facts are squarely faced, spanking and slapping to discipline children provides an aggressive model for the child to emulate and teaches that violence is acceptable. If we are striving to raise children in a nonviolent atmosphere, corporal punishment does not seem to fit.

On the other hand, neither is permissiveness acceptable—especially when pleading and haranguing doesn't stop undesired behavior, but nothing further is done. Children soon learn that they can get away with most anything and concurrently their respect for their parents dwindles to contempt for such impotency to enforce limits. Discipline is necessary but there are alternatives to physical discipline. Stopping the undesired behavior, not responding to it, removing privileges, withholding approval, and rewarding good behavior all bring the desired result without encouraging violence or aggressiveness. A good axiom to remember is that discipline should be reasonable, related and respectful.

Children do need and even want limits, if for no other reason than to show them we care enough to be concerned over what they do. Many times our children have pushed us to the limits just to get attention. They need constant assurance that we do care, but that assurance should be given in a positive way. Just asking, "Are you being mean because I'm not paying attention to you?" often breaks down barriers and opens the way for a big hug. Spanking, on the other hand, is more often a release of our own frustration when we have not devoted enough time and thought to what is most effective for the child. During minor crises we have a choice of negative or positive reinforcement. We can take our parental responsibilities seriously and plan for these times so as to avoid our own frustrations, or we can resort to spanks and slaps which are usually spontaneous and inconsistent.

The manner in which we speak to children can also be violent. If our remarks are severely critical, downgrading and repeated often they can damage the child's confidence and good self image.

Admittedly, we have not always been successful in eliminating all corporal punishment. There were those unhappy occasions when we were too weak to find a better way to handle the situation, but fortunately those times progressively declined as we applied more patience. When we closely examine offensive behavior it turns out to be more often than not the child's subconscious way of asking for love and attention.

Looking at the other side of the punishment and reward coin, we have found that rewarding children for good behavior is more positive. Psychologists call this reinforcing desired behavior and it is much more pleasant for both parent and child. Rewarding children when they do something well, or even when they just do what is expected, or use their initiative and imagination, stimulates the child's development and fosters a good self-concept. The reward need not be material. Something as simple as praise is effective. In our home we often leave a complimentary note when the child has a clean room. It is essential, though, that material rewards be accompanied by praise so that our love comes through just as clearly as material gifts.

Discipline should also be aimed at teaching the child responsibility. As freedom to experiment is allowed, the degree of that freedom must be governed by the child's ability to accept the accompanying responsibility. In reverse, as children demonstrate responsibility, they should be rewarded by expansion of the limits. Mistakes can be expected and the challenge then is to help the youngster fail successfully by learning from the mistake without being overwhelmed by the failure. It is of course desirable to confine these "successful failures" to areas which are not too serious. In this regard it is good to remember that the earlier a child starts learning from mistakes, the less serious the making of mistakes will be. Overprotectiveness tends to delay the mistake-making phase until the areas of experimentation are more serious.

An example of such expanding of limits with acceptance of responsibility occurs when youngsters reach the age to drive a car. We have always felt it grossly irresponsible for parents simply to turn their sixteen-year-olds loose on the highway since most young people that age do not comprehend the responsibility of driving. Insurance company statistics unfortunately bear out that fact. Since we are fussy about this responsibility, it determines the extent which our children are allowed to operate the family car. Learning the mechanics of how an automobile works, especially when they want a car of their own, is part of our program to build responsible drivers. Whenever periodic maintenance is necessary we have them crawling in and out and under the vehicle to make the necessary checks and perform the required servicing.

Responsibility is also important in building family spirit. Being conscientious about work, returning borrowed items and following through with promises makes people show that they are dependable and trustworthy. Mutual trust becomes an essential ingredient of family community, and feelings of self-worth and belonging develop when any family member contributes a fair share. Feeling part of the act is vital to family spirit.

Responsibility also contributes to a semblance of order. Things in chaos are hard to understand, but when there is systematic consistency and a pattern can be recognized then understanding takes place. This in turn stimulates self-confidence and motivates a person to proceed farther, and as a result children learn to become self-starters. The cycle goes full circle for as they develop understanding and self-confidence children feel good about themselves and their family.

Remaining responsible in our constantly changing world requires a certain flexibility and the ability to adapt behavior as conditions warrant. This does not necessarily mean complying with the trends, and we have decided that drifting with fashion and fad is due in a large degree to an inability to make decisions. The key is to recognize when change is required. Responsible people uphold certain basic values but alter behavior as new insight is gained. They should not rationalize to accommodate desires on the one hand or be overscrupulous on the other.

To avoid these two extremes we have always challenged our children to be discriminating. There is nothing which is purely good or purely evil. A wise person learns to sift out the good. Take religion as an example. For many years we looked to the church as the infallible authority and neglected its mandate that we form our own conscience. In this sense we allowed the church to prescribe our behavior without recognizing our own responsibility to search for the truth. In essence, we thought we were being handed the full truth without any effort. Then we began to see truth in other Christian denominations and later we recognized it in the Hindu, Buddhist, Jewish and Muslim faiths. While this awakening was taking place we also began to perceive errors being practiced in our own denomination and in other faiths. Our choice then was to grasp the truth and reject the errors. To maintain some sense of spirituality we had to become discriminating and this meant we had to have confidence that, after much prayer and study, we could make valid judgments.

A good place to start teaching children to discriminate is in the traits of their friends. As society emphasizes the good-guys/bad-guys concept, we need to recognize that nobody is perfect. We all have a mixture of good and bad habits. This should be kept in mind as we humbly observe the behavior of others. Teaching children to make these distinctions between desirable and undesirable decisions enhances their understanding. Of course reacting against poor behavior by a person is not tantamount to rejecting the person. Besides recognizing and affirming good traits, young people can reinforce and validate one another. Learning to make value judgments will also strengthen them the rest of their lives.

One value judgment we have made regards the roles normally played in the family by father and mother, husband and wife. For the first 26 years of our marriage we followed the traditional roles—Bob worked as the breadwinner and Janet was the homemaker. In this capacity Bob was gone from early morning until evening and it fell on Janet to minister to the children's needs during the day. In many ways Bob was a stranger to the family because he was not able to be in tune with the intimate relationships—not unusual under such an arrangement.

After we severed ourselves from the war industry, our activities melded together. Janet took a part-time job. She returned before the children came home from school so she still saw as much of them as if she were home all day. The difference came in Bob's life since he began doing research and writing at home and thus sees much more of the youngsters.

Mark, our youngest, was barely three years old when we started this arrangement; consequently at first he was home alone with Bob much of the day. When Bob went to a meeting, Mark went along. There was a large pillow in the corner of Bob's study where Mark took his nap. Of our ten children he was the only one, when small, who would go as readily to Bob as to Janet for a problem or a hurt. Until we experienced this blending of roles, Bob did not realize how much he was missing while the children were growing up. Now we are convinced that the ideal situation allows parents to share the outside work so each has ample and approximately equal time with the children—and where at least one parent is with the pre-school children most of the time.

Let's face it, raising children is a long-term vocation which requires attention and long-range planning. It means being constantly alert to changing developments and coping with today's technological age geared toward instant gratification. We are an impatient people and would like immediate results but this rarely happens with children who require a lot of patience and much plan-ning. There is one great source of encouragement—when we set our mind to doing our very best there is always a higher force which makes us more successful than we could otherwise be. Yet practicing love and nonviolence in the intimate family relationship is the most grueling test. There can be no facades. If it is not real, it won't fly in a family. Fortunately we do not have to appear infalli-ble. Children understand when they see parents strug-gling to overcome human weaknesses. In fact, the most potent example we can set for our children is the let them see us searching for the right priorities and striving to live accordingly.

All families have the potential for being a spirited com-munity that has a healthy effect on society. That potential must be consciously cultivated. Little events happen every day. Joys and sorrows, successes and failures can all become a binding force if they are shared together. It is the small things which add up to a tremendous impact. We merely have to be aware of them and bring them to the consciousness of the family community for sharing.

3

Authority

O! What authority and show of truth
Can cunning sin cover itself withal.
—*William Shakespeare*
Much Ado About Nothing

Truth is the secret of eloquence and
of virtue, the basis of moral authority;
it is the highest summit of art and of life.
—*Henri Frederick Amiel*
Journal 1883

We once witnessed a flagrant abuse of parental authority. A father and small son were walking ahead of us in the variety store. The boy spied a toy on the floor, picked it up and started to place it on the shelf. Presumably embarrassed that his son had handled merchandise without asking, the father roared to put it down. People stared and the youngster started to sob, at which time the father gave the boy a swat and told him to stop crying. When the boy tried to place the toy on the shelf the father yelled to put it back on the floor where he found it. It was obvious to us that this father expected unquestioning response to his authority.

A popular bumper sticker calls us to Question Authority. It is good because it makes us think and it is good to think. Amid all the violence of today's world we must remain painfully aware of such revelations as the Winter Soldiers' Testimony, the Pentagon Papers and Watergate. These are just a sampling of cases which have worn the authenticity of our so-called authorities very thin. Within the last couple of decades we have probably seen a greater credibility gap in authority than at any time in history. It can be seen how sin has, in Shakespeare's words, cloaked itself in authority and a show of truth. At this very moment alert minds can recognize evil and corruption disguised as truth coming from the experts.

The shibboleth Question Authority signals an awakening, particularly among young people who are fed up with promises of a future that never happens. But the problem is not so much in questioning the authority of self-styled experts at leading government as in bringing that analysis home to the family. In the context of a parent's responsibility to children, Webster defines authority as "the right to expect obedience," and goes on to describe it as a "delegated power over others."

If we pursue this secular definition there are two phrases which stand out: right and delegated power. We parents have the right to expect obedience from our children because we are responsible for their care and upbringing. Too often the realization stops at that point with no further thought as to the context of parent-child relationships in the exercise of that right. Parents feel that inherent in the act of begetting or adopting children they gain control over their lives. This attitude can work to the parents' satisfaction when the kids are small, but when the teen years are reached rebellion usually sets in. Authoritarian parents are so commonplace in our culture that teenage rebellion is considered natural—which it is, under the circumstances. But rebellion, when it does occur to test limits and form values, need not be so intense. Furthermore, when youngsters reject misused authority they often cast out what is good along with the bad. Psychological development can be set back years and even decades.

So what is the correct use of parental authority? A good rule to remember is that where a right is granted there is always an accompanying responsibility—which is often misinterpreted or overlooked. Parents have the responsibility to use such authority correctly and in the manner and for the purpose for which it was granted. Parents are not to be slave masters. They are to provide knowledge and guidance. Neither are parents infallible. Even when vested with parental authority we can, and often do, err. We should admit that. And when we talk about a right being granted we ask: "From whom?" That brings us to the second phrase—delegated power.

Our true authority as parents comes from God. It is given to us to use in fulfilling our commitment to God, to each other and to the children God entrusts in our care. It is vital that we keep this straight; for God is the only true authority and we are allowed, as the earthly parents of God's children, real or adopted, to be the instruments of God's work. Jesus described this phenomenon when he said it was not on his own authority that he speaks, but on the authority of the father who speaks through him. As parents we need to be acutely alert to letting God speak and act through us to our children. We need a humble awareness that on our own we have no credibility whatsoever. Forgetting where our authority comes from really messes things up.

This authority which flows through us from God is an authority of love. Love permits freedom. Love is demonstrated through service. Love is based on truth. Our delegated power over our children is the power to free them, the power to serve them and the power to show them the truth. This is the power of love which can flow through us from God.

An erroneous concept of the Ten Commandments reduces it essentially to a list of DOs and DON'Ts. Compliance is motivated by the fear of hell (punishment) and the promise of heaven (reward)—not a lofty motivation since it is based upon serving our own best interests. This distortion tends to be a Christian problem since in Judaism the Ten Commandments have more depth. Doing certain things and refraining from others out of personal considerations is better than nothing, but it is restrictive and does not allow us to exercise our full potential. Nevertheless, this punishment and reward system is essentially the basis on which most authority still works today.

When some 2,000 years ago Jesus introduced, or reintroduced, the law of love, the rules remained the same, but compliance shifted from self-concern to a desire to please God. This compassion transcends ego-centered concerns and is centered on love for God, and loving God through our neighbors in this world. Such love is liberating and positive—an aspiration to perfection because pure love is perfect. In his gospel, John equates love to God—"God is Love." Therefore love is perfect because God is perfect. When we love we share the authority of God.

Applying this reasoning to the authority delegated to us as parents, we see that every decision we make and every action we perform for our children needs to be done with a sincere and caring love. It is totally opposite that pseudo authority of rulers who subject slaves, albeit through kindly treatment that allows the slaves to be quite fond of their rulers. Rather, it is the authority which prepares our children for independence. In that sense it is a temporary authority which allows freedom to experiment as responsibility for that experimentation is accepted by the child.

Because this authority of love fosters freedom, parents should respect the free will of their children just as God respects ours when he offers help and guidance (grace) while not forcing us to accept it. Our duty as parents is to form and guide our children to where they can eventually use their free will in a responsible manner. Children should have freedom offered to them as early as possible, in degrees commensurate with their age and ability. The only time parents should impose their own judgment is when the children are in danger through lack of knowledge or experience, but every intervention should be exercised with loving sensitivity, and only for as long as needed. If intervention is not gradually withdrawn as the child matures, parents venture into the area of over-protectiveness—which is the main cause of rebellion. It is well to remember that some day we will not be able to intervene when our children are in danger. For that reason, if for none other, we should prepare them for each step of independence as soon as they can handle it. To an increasing degree, according to their ability to reason, children should be allowed free will in accepting or rejecting our guidance. They will make mistakes and it is our function to help them fail successfully.

If we were perfect enough to exercise God's authority of love in its purest sense there would be no disharmony in our family. Natural disagreements would arise, as well as questioning and challenging, but not rebellion as such. This of course is a theoretical ideal and we have to allow for our human weaknesses. In our family we have not yet been able to completely eliminate punishment and reward with all their accompanying lack of perfection. Nonetheless, the perfect authority of love should be our aspiration. As we move closer to that ideal, the need to punish and reward with material things diminishes, so the giving of material gifts becomes a manifestation of love rather than something motivated by behavior.

Corporal punishment is an important subject because it is so widely practiced. Resorting to physical punishment is at the violent extreme of the punishment and reward scale. As the practice of spanking continues, it becomes more convenient for the parents to spank than to exercise the patience needed to work out a better solution. Meanwhile the child, rather than learning right from wrong, is guided by fear of punishment. When insensitivity to punishment sets in, children often do bad things presuming that the subsequent spanking will cancel out the wrong. If our goal is to stimulate good judgment in our children rather than teach blind obedience to authority, spanking and slapping are not the means to that end.

As a medium for the flow of God's love, our vocation as parents becomes a life of service. As Jesus washed the feet of his disciples, we too are the servants of our children. Parents realize this in a physical sense but not so readily in the authoritative sense. To prepare children for independence our exercise of authority must be subject to the needs of our children in all aspects of their personality. When we give advice we must be certain it is the guidance the child really needs in that particular instance. Granting or refusing a request should be for the child's benefit and not to enhance our own prestige or peace of mind. Most of all, we have to remain constantly aware that we are not an authority in our own right.

An authority of love is based on truth. Mohandas Gandhi said he could make no distinction between God and truth—"Truth is God." In the same vein, our authority as parents is also an authority of truth. Not that we become infallible, quite the contrary, but because we are so fallible and influenced by pride and ego, we must struggle and pray unceasingly for God's truth and love to show through us. That means we have to live the truth. No double standards, no do-as-I-say-not-as-I-do slogans, because that is living a lie. Parenthood is a TOTAL commitment. We will make mistakes and it is very important to admit those mistakes, especially to our children. They know we are not perfect. In the long run they will have more love and respect for us when they see us struggling—sometimes failing, sometimes suc ceeding—to reach our ideal. Seeing our human side is a powerful modeling which in the end will encourage them to struggle with us.

Learning is not a one-way street. We parents can learn a lot from our children. Several years ago Bob overstepped his authority when correcting Mary, who later left him the following note:

> Dad, you don't have to be right all the time. You're just human like everyone else. If you make a mistake you're not going to lose your "father figure" with us. You don't have to put on the "perfect father act" because we do respect you when you're yourself (not so uptight and worried that if you don't scare us then you're not going to have control over us). But you will because we think of you as our "human father" that makes mistakes, and who we forgive and have respect for. We still love you very much, just like we always have, ever since you used to push us around in a baby buggy.
>
> Love always and forever.
> Mary

You can imagine how moving that note was to Bob who also recognized that he had allowed his ego to choke off the flow of truth and love from God. To properly use our authority as teacher and guide through our children's formative years it is essential to their development, possibly even their salvation, that that flow from God continue unabated. It is our prime responsibility as parents to keep the channels clear to allow that flow. The closer we can come to perfection in submitting to God's will, the more enlightened children we will raise. They, in turn, will have a significant impact on society.

The incident that caused Mary to write that note resulted when Bob let his emotions interfere with good judgment. In his own childhood he had experienced a completely different spirit of fairness from his dad (actually his stepfather, since his father had been killed in an auto accident during Bob's infancy). For some reason, when Bob was growing up he decided to test how fair his father would be with him. One evening at the dinner table his dad was reprimanding him for shoddy table manners. Hardly before he stopped scolding, Bob asked to use the family car that night. His father mulled it over for a few seconds and then consented. His displeasure with Bob's crude behavior at the dinner table did not influence the fairness of his consideration of the request. That incident developed a lot of confidence in Bob regarding his father's fairness.

As we parents become more successful in exercising an authority of love we begin to earn our children's respect instead of having to demand it. At this point, it is good for them to "question authority" because then they will accept our example as a model for their lives. When children find the authority oppressive they will rebel. Rebellion is a struggle to overcome the restrictions which inhibit growth—an attempt to expand limits. In that sense a certain degree of rebellion can serve a benevolent function, but it can turn dangerous if unjust limits are not relaxed. In many respects we parents are too emotionally involved with our children to always recognize when more freedom is deserved. We tend to view them as our small darlings long after they are able to shift for themselves. At such times rebellion can be a warning to reevaluate our handling of the situation and we may have to back down when we realize that our own fears and prejudices are preventing God's authority to shine. Such backing down is not losing face. It is showing responsible behavior in correcting an admitted mistake.

Sometimes we become so involved in our parenting responsibilities that we take our children for granted. This practice was brought to our attention one day when

Diane, eleven at the time, wrote this poem:

> People might not have cars.
> People might not have jewelry.
> People might not have lots of things,
>   but I've never known a person
>   who does not have feelings.
> Every person in this world has feelings.

Parents can get a lot of feedback on how well they are performing from messages like this. Written notes are great for conveying thoughts more precisely because more thoughtful consideration usually goes into preparing them than into speaking. Also, the receiver pays more attention to them. Another meaningful message came in 1969 when Bob received a birthday card from our oldest daughter, Janie, 20 at the time. Janie had made the card herself and used a verse she'd found:

> The teacher who walks in the shadow
> of the temple, among his followers,
> gives not of his wisdom but rather
> of his faith and lovingness.

> If he is indeed wise he does not bid
> you enter the house of his wisdom,
> but rather leads you to the
> threshold of your own mind.

This verse might have veiled a barbed hint or a recognition of our struggle to practice loving authority, but we were then helping to prepare an adult discussion session on authority and we discussed it quite a bit at home. Janie was undoubtedly responding to some of those conversations.

More recently Janet received a handmade vase of God-made flowers from Mary and Diane with this note attached:

> You've made us so happy
> By being the beautiful person
>   that you are.
> Your love and understanding
>   are so important to us.
> We are very fortunate to have
>   you as a mother.

Happy Birthday.
    Flowers from Mary
    Vase from Diane
    Ourselves from you.
    Thank you.

The verse from Janie emphasized faith and lovingness. The one from Diane and Mary pointed to love and understanding. These are the attributes to which children respond most readily. They foster the respect which opens the way for learning. Love is the threshold of truth and the happy part of the whole picture is that showing love is the most pleasant act a parent can perform.

It is not always clear, however, in what manner an expression of love is best perceived. It should naturally be offered in a way which suits each individual child because children relate in different ways. During one period Kathy and Teri were at a point where one would accuse the other of not being sorry for some deed. We finally recognized that Kathy was not able to feel contrition from Teri because Teri said she was sorry but her actions didn't show it. On the other hand, Kathy would convey her regrets through a kind deed but Teri did not recognize them unless they were verbalized. Each was responding to the other according to her own ability to perceive and communication was not taking place. When we pointed out what was happening they began responding according to the other's ability to perceive and the communication problem diminished remarkably. It is the same with showing and sensing love. There are many methods, and discovering the proper one for the given time and person is extremely important.

Even though it may not be possible to completely eliminate the punishment and reward system, it is important to exercise it with a visible display of love. Punishment is recognition for being naughty and reward is recognition for being good. But love is recognition for just being, and that is the most important recognition of all for the child.

Let us not forget that bumper sticker telling us to Question Authority. It applies most of all to us parents. Let us continually question our own authority—how we exercise it and express it and with what purpose. Let us frequently ask ourselves if we are really an instrument through which flows the love, freedom, service and truth which God sends. This questioning, in the final sense, may be the most important thing we can do for our children.

4

The Formative Years

The little world of childhood with its familiar
surroundings is a model of the greater world. The
more intensively the family has stamped its character
upon the child, the more it will tend to feel and see
its earlier miniature world again in the bigger world
of adult life.

—*Carl Gustav Jung*
The Theory of Psychoanalysis (1913)

Nine-year-old David slinked into the Loaves and Fishes
Family Kitchen behind his parents and immediately hid
beneath a table. He cowered like an animal as our
daughter Diane, a volunteer working with the children,
approached him. The kitchen supervisor explained that,
although his family relationships had now changed for
the better, David still suffered the psychological effects of
brutality and was living in an automobile with his mother,
stepfather and five younger children. He was being
treated much more kindly by his stepfather, but his youth
was still overshadowed by past experiences as well as the
imposed responsibility of supervising younger brothers
and sisters.

Diane felt challenged to overcome David's timidity. She
spoke quietly to him on the three days a week the kitchen
served meals. Gradually she was able to coax him into
some of the children's games but he was wary and
reserved. This went on for several months until summer
day camp commenced. Under these conditions Diane was
able to work with David every day and for longer periods
of time. Gradually his reticence diminished.

A beach trip was scheduled for the midpoint of the day
camp period. It was during this experience that David,
relieved of responsibility for younger siblings, really

opened up. His robust participation in play belied a previous psychological handicap—he was very much just an ordinary boy having a very good time. Diane related that this was a turning point as David accepted the others and felt accepted by them.

On the last day of this summer activity Diane was leading a group of small children down the hall when she heard the patter of running feet from behind. She turned just as David grabbed her with a big hug which Diane described as having a special plea for affection. He then scampered off with the other chidren.

David's story illustrates two effects on children. First is that violence experienced during the early years has a devastating effect on a child's character. As we shall discuss below, it is the lack of love which produces a violent personality. Second, the experience with David epitomizes the redeeming effect of compassion and recognition. When Diane treated him with caring feelings he gradually came out of his shell—the shell in which brooding festers violence. He became accepted as someone of value and that led to his own acceptance of peers in his small world. It is this acceptance and belonging which leads to nonviolence in interpersonal relations.

People fill a spectrum between many personality extremes—quiet to boisterous, solemn to frivolous, sincere to perfidious, serene to tumultuous. True, heredity is partly responsible for this variety of characteristics, especially as our environment becomes more impregnated with substances affecting genetics, but the bulk of character formation takes place in the home. The child's basic attitudes and beliefs are molded within the family atmosphere where, unfortunately, much of what children are absorbing today is not wholesome. It is critical that parents recognize this situation and correct it. More precisely, our parental duty is to provide an atmosphere whereby our children can experiment in a wide range of activities to develop their unique personalities. When such an atmosphere is provided amid visible love we can be pretty certain that good traits will follow. Doing the right thing at the prescribed time isn't as important as doing the best we can with love and with a sincere concern for what is best for the child.

Parents tread dangerously close to mind manipulation when they do what they think is best for the child. What we should really strive for is an open mind for both ourselves and the child. Failing that we are truly manipulating the child's development to conform to our own sense of values no matter how unintentional that may be. Quite frequently we aspire to values we do not actually practice. When this happens the duplicity is not missed by the child. In later years youngsters may rebel against our vocalized ideas but, more often than not, they will emulate the example we actually live.

We only have to look about us to see the results of poor character formation. High pressure advertising and our self-image as consumers fosters the traits of craving, competitiveness and greed. The outcome is frequently a fixation on acquiring property with less attention being given to the well-being of other people. This set of circumstances can be recognized in the chain of causation taught by Eastern religions:

Craving gives rise to pursuit of gain.
Pursuit of gain gives rise to desire and passion.
Desire and passion give rise to tenacity.
Tenacity gives rise to possession.
Possession gives rise to avarice and more possessions.
Avarice and more possessions lead to keeping watch and ward over possessions.
Many bad and wicked things arise from keeping watch and ward over possessions: blows, wounds, strife, quarreling, slander, lies.
This is the chain of causation. If there were no craving would there arise pursuit of gain, desire and passion, tenacity, love of possessions and avarice for more possessions?
If there would not be love of private possessions would there not be peace?

Buddha spoke those words over 25 centuries ago but they still very accurately depict conditions in developed countries today. What is described is violence and the last two questions pose the prescription for a nonviolent personality. The formation of such a personality starts in the family during early childhood.

Just because a newborn baby has not mastered control of its body does not mean those early years are not important. Development of the child's personality begins at birth, if not before. Hospital-born infants leave the warmth, comfort and security of their mothers' wombs to enter a world of glaring lights and banging utensils. Such a debut could be a major contributing factor to many of today's neurotic ailments.

One might argue that there is no scientific proof of this early cause-effect relationship. Perhaps not. We haven't taken the time or devoted the resources to really study those facets. Our scientific community, the most formidable in the world, is too busy developing new ways of making money or waging war. There is little talent left over for determining causes and cures for social problems. So if we wait for scientific proof before we search for less violent ways of birthing and parenting, we may be sitting on our hands for a long time. We parents need to act on our gut feelings in probing for the truth. We need the self-confidence that we are qualified to determine what is best for our children.

Such self-confidence has revived the custom of giving birth at home amid love and tenderness. This was the case with our granddaughter, Hannah. Our daughter Mary and her husband Gene wanted their baby to receive a loving and joyful welcome into this world. During Mary's pregnancy they both took courses and studied the art of birthing. When the time drew near, they had made arrangements for hospital care if complications should arise. In Hannah's case the birth was normal.

It is true that some births need medical and surgical help but that does not mean that all childbirths have to take place in production line fashion, accomplished by impersonal shift workers. Medical help and guidance are important, but should be just that. The ideal situation is when the parents and the doctor recognize the scope and the limits of their respective functions and fulfill them accordingly.

Our state legislator recounted how one of his staff was reading Frederick Laboyer's Birth Without Violence while in the obstetrician's waiting room. When the doctor saw the book he dismissed it as a lot of garbage. Asked why, he responded: "Because our society is violent and the first chance we have to teach the kid that, the better." If we adopt that defeatist attitude we will be whipped before we get started. It is wrong to imply that humanity is violent by nature. Violence stems from greed and craving which has been fostered over the centuries and is a deeply entrenched plague which has been handed down from parent to child for generations. Today violence is spreading havoc because there has been no serious effort to reverse the momentum.

A better choice does exist—the nonviolence of love which springs from spiritual roots. Humans do possess a strong drive to seek friends and love others and this is nowhere more visible than in children. Focusing on this nonviolent and loving nature could well lead to the cure for society's problems. When we shoulder responsibility and cease looking for others to lead the way, we can start the practice of nonviolence within ourselves first, and then in our family community. This is not easy, but it certainly has a fulfilling potential.

The family's prime role in fostering nonviolence in children was highlighted in the 1982 report of the California Commission on Crime Control and Violence Prevention. Its lead paragraph states that "most current approaches to violence address its symptoms . . . looking for better ways to fish bodies out of the river while failing to repair the bridge." The commission emphasized rather: "There is nothing inevitable about the level of violence we currently experience. The United States ranks most violent among Western, industrialized democracies . . . because certain aspects of our social and cultural condition encourage violence. This fact holds realistic hope for a less violent future." In like manner the United States Attorney General's Task Force on Violent Crime concluded that "the wave of serious violent crime reflects a breakdown of the social order, not the legal order."

The California report, in its findings, places parenting, early childhood development and family violence as the first item of priority. It states that "no social institution is more fundamental to an individual's development, and thus to an understanding of the roots of violent behavior, than the family." The report explains that it is in family life that a youngster first learns (or fails to learn) the values, rules, attitude and skills necessary to function constructively in society. Within the family a person acquires a sense of self and the self's worth, forming the basic human bonds which are so important in determining subsequent social relations. All of this acknowledges that the family is the basic unit of society.

We have had many happy moments watching our children grow and develop and experiment to meet the mysteries of the world. Yet how easy easy it is to start taking our children for granted, becoming unintentionally exploitative. Sometimes we become so caught up in the routine of day-to-day living that we ask them to run trifling errands and perform menial tasks for our convenience. This your-legs-are-younger-than-mine attitude is often justified as teaching the kids responsibility. What they are actually taught is to get someone else to do as many of the undesirable jobs as possible. As parents we should be alert to this misuse of our authority which mandates that a true sense of responsibility be taught within a framework of loving and sharing. Responsibility is not something acquired through a discipline of exercises and chores. It is something which evolves out of love for others. Carrying their fair share of the load is important but it should not be done in an atmosphere of servitude.

We have found that it is important that our children be aware of the work we parents do around the home. Simply having our names on the chores list stimulates an atmosphere of sharing. In our family it works something like this: the children take turns caring for pets and doing some of the weekly cleaning. They also rotate with Bob at washing dishes. Janet cooks and tends the garden. Everyone takes care of their own room. Bob does the clothes washing and car servicing, and the children learn by helping him with house repairs. There is a certain amount of flexibility as well as spontaneous interplay such as with car work, cooking and gardening. At times there is some griping, but the younger ones do realize that everyone is carrying a fair share of the load.

Most parents are not intentionally exploitative but just become a little careless at times in fulfilling their mission. The effect, however, is the same. Later when the kids reach adolescence we dismiss rebellion as normal, but not many of us seek to understand the roots of dissent. When we exercise our authority as a genuine caring service, which prepares them for independence by giving them increasing freedom to experiment as they demonstrate responsibility, there may be normal differences of opinion but not revolt. Dissension surfaces when we retard that experimentation or become over-protective. In many areas of our interest—such as golf, bowling, etc.—we desire perfection so much that we practice unceasingly. Why not strive for that same perfection as parents. The stakes are much higher, but then, so is the satisfaction.

At the beginning of each school year we are overwhelmed at the lists of regulations which are sent home for parents to read and sign. This has become necessary because so many children do not have respect for others. There seems to be a "thou shalt not " for every eventuality. Just as we mentally revolt against this cascade of decrees, we find ourselves reacting in the same way as the children do when we make all-encompassing rules rather than teach them to be aware of circum stances and discriminate between right and wrong.

Once Bob told the family that when he was in the third grade a friend of his was blinded by a thrown rock. From that time on rock throwing was taboo and severe penalties were given for tossing stones at school. That memory stayed with Bob and the rule was passed on to our family. Years later when Mark was about three we were strolling along a mountain stream when Mark picked up a pebble. Bob started to caution him about throwing it but, as he admitted later, glimpsing Mark's boyish enthusiasm stopped him. Certainly there was no danger in chucking pebbles into the water here. Naturally schools have to prohibit rock throwing for the safety of others but that is also true of bows and arrows. Yet there are archery ranges where shooting arrows can be enjoyed safely when certain precautions are practiced. Why shouldn't rock tossers have that same opportunity?

Admittedly, it is more time consuming to teach a child when and where it is safe to chuck rocks than to forbid the activity entirely. Nevertheless, it is our parental duty to teach our children how to reason and think. In talking this incident out Bob recalled how he used to revel in clandestine rock throwing, often under rather tenuous safety conditions. Thus it seemed that taking advantage of Mark's ability to reason would be the healthiest choice in the long run. It is also more fun. Sometimes the whole family enjoys splashing rocks into the water when there is no danger of hurting anyone. It also fosters a good relationship among us.

Good relationships with parents have a powerful influence on the children. That, of course, really starts with the relationship between parents. Given the divorce rate statistics in this country, this vital cornerstone of parenting is slipping in crumbling mortar. Even in those families that do stick together, the bond between mother and father is often one of coexistence rather than dynamic love and respect. We frequently fall into the bad habit of taking each other for granted when we get caught up in routine. It is a terrible source of anxiety for children to see their two most loved human beings bickering and exchanging subtle insults.

Naturally, family life is not all harmony. Parents can and do have disagreements but it is how these disagreements are handled that is important. When we react emotionally without thinking, it worries our children. Even minor disagreements can appear to the children as major combat. The tone of voice and the inflections which the child picks up are more important than the actual words uttered—they may not even understand what the argument is all about but the vibrations get through. If the conflict is going to relieve pent up emotions, the parents should retire into privacy and out of earshot.

On the other hand, if the parents can talk it out while showing respect and concern for each other, this sets a good example to practice in front of the children. There is no better way to learn how to handle conflict than to see it successfully resolved by parents.

Since actions speak louder than words, the father who admonishes his children to respect the law and then asks them to watch for cops out the back window as he speeds along the highway is teaching his children a double standard. They will obviously learn not to be too scrupulous about the law if they can keep from being caught. Likewise, to teach nonviolence in the home we must strive to practice it ourselves. Too often we are quick with irritated speech and action when angry. This exhibits violence. Again using the automobile as an analogy, the manner in which children see us interacting with other drivers is a potent lesson in either exercising violence or struggling for nonviolence and cooperation. There is little that escapes the sharp and curious eyes of our youngsters.

As models for our children we must remember that they are going to imitate our actions. Even though they may become aloof during their adolescent years, it is the behavior they learn at home which they will practice for the rest of their lives. Children identify with the parents who raise them whether they be natural or adopted, whether those parents encourage it or not. It is important that the identity be a good one and that the children have a feeling of being wanted, appreciated and loved, and that they are able to return that love.

The vocation of parenting is absolutely vital to our society. Parenthood is taken much too lightly today, yet the molding and forming of a human being is the most important responsibility one can imagine. Parents may be willing to die for their children, but too few of them are willing to sacrifice enough to be really willing to live for them.

Sacrifice is not a comfortable word in our vocabulary. It immediately conjures up images of hair shirts and giving up pleasures. The emphasis today is on seeking comfort and not giving up anything except the throwaways we tire of. But sacrifice has a positive aspect—allowing ourselves to be God's instruments in creating a human personality. This means offering a portion of ourselves through caring for and nurturing the little ones. Sacrifice can be equated to love and without love our children will suffer. In the final sense, sacrifice is letting

God's love flow through us to our children. Parental sacrifice is a joy once parents recognize wholesome values and priorities and, above all, meaningful goals.

Such loving sacrifice allows children to identify in a positive way with their parents and maintain a feeling of security. There is no secure feeling without sensing love. Without love and the security of family unity the child will not develop a healthy personality. Raising an insecure youngster without love is raising a psychological invalid.

Years ago Sister Paulina Mary, a Catholic nun and child psychologist, talked to a Christian Family Movement convention on the topic of developing a healthy personality in youngsters. This talk has been an inspiration to us during our child raising years for she emphasized to us the important role of parents in developing healthy personalities in their children. In her view the aspects of a child's developing personality come both from within through heredity and without, chiefly from the mother and father. That is very, very important. Although peer groups and teachers contribute to a child's personality development, most happens in the home. Understanding and reflecting on how the collection of personalities form society, we can see how important family life is in determining the warp and woof of the greater community.

Sister Paulina Mary also stressed the goal of personality development in a child as self-realization or self-actualization—to make real or actual the potentiality within them, and itemized five levels of personality development, in increasing order of importance:

1) Physical,
2) Psychological (both intellectual and emotional),
3) Social,
4) Moral,
5) Spiritual or religious.

The goal is to integrate these five aspects so one does not dominate or conflict with the others. As we move down the list in increasing importance, the visibility diminishes because in our society the higher, less important attributes get the most attention. Nevertheless, for a balanced personality all five must interact harmoniously

to develop a feeling of worth. We feel good about ourselves when we have a good self-concept. Again, as
pointed out in the California study, self-esteem is
indispensable to a nonviolent personality.

Thus it is so important that we parents strive to
promote a good self-concept in our children. Self-esteem
can be stimulated by helping children trust the parents as
well as themselves. Consequently, consistency is important, especially in discipline. If something is allowed
yesterday and refused today the youngsters become
confused and lose confidence in their judgment of right
and wrong. Likewise there should be consistency
between what is right and wrong for both parents and
children. It cannot be right, for instance, for a parent to
use profane language and wrong for the children to do
so.

Developing this good self-concept—this good picture
of oneself—is of supreme importance in integrating a
harmonious personality in a child. A child will learn to
ask: "Am I the kind of person who does that?" In this
regard, self-esteem is the foundation of morality because
it guides what we do and how we do it. On the other
hand, once a child develops a poor self-image it is very
hard to change. People will distort reality to justify the
view they have of themselves and learn to be comfortable
with a poor self-concept.

We were distorting reality ourselves when Bob was a
missile engineer. We played all kinds of mental games to
justify our source of income. Eventually we exhausted
these "mechanisms of moral self-deception," as one
insightful person called them, and faced the reality that
nuclear weapons are made to destroy people, and
depending on them for protection was a spiritual danger.
As with an alcoholic, so it was with our concept of
respectable citizensonly when we were able to face the
truth could we begin to revise our living pattern. We
human beings are very addicted to rabid patriotism and
money-making. We are still struggling to bring our social
and emotional levels into harmony with the moral and
spiritual.

A good self-concept must meet two criteria: 1) it must fit
what we really are, and 2) it must be a picture of oneself

doing good things. Thus it is important that as parents we emphasize the positive in our children, diligently looking for and lauding their good traits, no matter how difficult they may be to recognize or how trivial that trait may seem. This is also helpful when correcting children. Rather than saying, "You are always leaving your coat on the floor?" we could say, "I am surprised that you are so careless." In this way we help the children to see that they are perceived as thoughtful persons who would put their coats away.

Lastly we would like to stress how important it is to help children accept what they actually are. Acceptance of self is a fundamental part of good interpersonal relationships, both in the family and later in society. If John is a deaf child who has to wear a hearing aid, that is something he must be helped to accept. Accepting his handicap without learning how to cope with it, however, is complacency. By learning how to communicate better with people through sign language and lip reading, and by learning the best response to people who do not speak clearly, then he is not being complacent, but learns to be responsible for himself with the faculties he has. This is the basis of good mental health in our children but it requires a lot of awareness and work on our part. In this same manner, those personality traits on the less visible end of the character spectrum must receive due attention.

To discover whether there is a parallel between mind manipulation and personality formation we must look at our emphasis and purpose. There is a difference between helping a child in actualizing potentiality and molding a youngster to predetermined standards. There is also a difference between allowing them to experiment with their own ideas and negligently turning them loose without adequate guidance. These are important distinctions for a parent to recognize and it is not always easy to do so. The best approach, we have found, is with an unselfish and loving respect for the youngster's individuality.

5

Guns and War Toys

The woods are made for the
   hunter of dreams,
The brooks for the fishers of song;
To the hunter who hunts for the
   gunless game
The streams and wood belong.
   —*Sam Walter Foss*
      The Bloodless Sportsman

Mark is a great guy. He enjoys life and likes all people, dogs, horses and giraffes. He is the most popular cowboy on the block. Sporting a red hat, bandanna and leather vest, a gun will flash into his hand at a whisper. Corks will bombard the living room when an Indian uprising takes place. Television has taught Mark much about Indians and guns. Dad says guns should never be pointed at people—never! This strange advice is hard to understand while the A-Team knocks off its enemies with impunity.

Thus was our son Mark at the age of three.

One day this saddle bum comes in from the back yard corral, tugs a chair up to the table with one foot and commands the barkeep: "Gimme some beer!"

"What?" gasps Mother before she recovers enough to pour a glass of milk. Yes, it is hard for a young cowpoke to get the hang of things in this world.

Another day at the shopping center with Mom and Dad, Mark hears the loud speaker blare that Indians will be dancing in the mall. "Indians! WOW! And here I am without my six-shooter," panics Mark. "What will I do?"

What to do is decided for Mark as Dad tugs his hand, saying: "Come on cowboy. Let's go watch."

Mark would really rather not but how can he resist with Dad towing him toward the mall.

"The Indians are good, Mark," comforts Dad as he senses the cowboy's reluctance. "They are just like everyone else except on special occasions they wear brilliant costumes and headdresses."

Mark feels better, but it's still hard to adjust what Dad says to what he sees on TV.

"Who-oo-py! Ki Yi Yi!" Boom! Boom! The tom-toms beat out a thunderous tempo and wild shrieks fill the air. As Mark recovers and peeks out from behind Dad's legs he is having second thoughts about this situation. His mind is reeling, "Why don't Mom and Dad run for cover? We'll get shot full of arrows any minute."

"The dance is beginning," says Dad, nudging Mark toward the center. "Let's get up front where we can see."

"This is certainly the end," worries Mark. "That Indian music is exciting though, and the dancers look like they're having fun. Maybe it will be safe as long as they don't have bows and arrows. Besides, the Indian kids look friendly."

Soon Mark is completely entranced with the dancing and music. During a rest Dad takes him over to meet Chief Bold Eagle. "Howdy, cowboy," greets the chief. "Let's make-um peace."

Mark gingerly shakes hands, and then his grip firms; shyness disappears. The Indians are now his blood brothers.

Many ideas race through Mark's drowsy head on the way home. "Gee, Mom and Dad are right. I wonder where they get all those dopey TV stories."

Introducing children to experiences where they can see reality and relate to actual people, rather than the concepts so readily promoted on television, is a superb means of educating them to what the real world is all about. TV has become a powerful medium in our generation and that power is far from being all good, for the TV has invaded the home and competes heavily with other means of personality formation. This is epitomized in children's fascination with guns, shooting and war toys. In our family we have done much experimenting with this aspect of parenting and our thinking has gone through several stages.

Our oldest children always had cap pistols and squirt guns—water pistols are really fun on a hot summer day. As they grew older we bought B-B guns and .22 caliber rifles. Safety precautions began with the toy replicas and were carried over to the real thing. The children reached the height of ecstasy on those occasions when we took the 12-gauge shotgun out for skeet shooting. Rifles often accompanied us on camping trips as those outings afforded opportunity to enjoy a little sharpshooting. All our children had fun as their turn came at "picking off the cans." Target practice meant exactly that, not destroying wildlife—except possibly for ground squirrels which carry disease and cause soil erosion from their burrowing. (Later we stopped even that wanton killing because we recognized those reasons as merely excuses to shoot at living creatures.) Hunting was once Bob's favorite sport and the boys loved to tag along with him— killing animals to eat was not the same as shooting something for the fun of it, or so we deluded ourselves at the time.

In recent years a new philosophy has slowly enveloped us. We are attempting to lay aside old practices and obsolete thinking which no longer have meaning as far as valuing life is concerned. We started experimenting with new ideas because, after several years of resisting brutality at the social level, the concept of nonviolence was turning inward to touch our personal values. We saw that nonviolence must start in the family if we are ever to reach a social structure devoid of violence. We read, attended seminars, and discussed this subject with others. A statement by Dr. William C. Morris influenced us:

> We must be very afraid of aggression, and we must be very afraid of it in ourselves. . . We're afraid when children express aggression. . . You've got to under-stand, talk these things out—the aggression and difference of style—because they are always in the picture.

> The affective life, which is the substance of socialization, is there all the time. You cannot avoid it, you can

repress it, you can ignore it, [but children] are learning patterns about themselves and other people; roles are being taught by conditions.

What a child learns from us is far less from our words than from our behavior. If we are to teach children to manage their aggression, we will start out by managing our own.

[*Peace Education in the Pre-School Years*, edited by Maryellen G. Hadjisky and Florence B. Stroll (Detroit: Wayne State University, 1972) p. 12]

We as a people, particularly in developed countries, are very responsive when we are told we must be afraid. Fear was exactly our response to Dr. Morris' admonition. We became very protective. Without even realizing it at the time, we were doing exactly what we were warned against. We were repressing aggression and ignoring the stimulation of society on the kids. In our panic we missed the whole message of Dr. Morris' statement.

When our son Mark was born we decided that he would be raised differently. He would not play with war toys or guns—period! This decision seemed all the more poignant since Dr. Benjamin Spock had revised his famous manual Baby and Child Care in this regard, explaining that he used to pooh-pooh the forbidding of play guns but pointed out that about age three or four the child develops a fascination for these instruments. Now he advises telling the child who asks for a gun, "I want people to love each other. I don't believe in guns so I won't buy you a gun."

Dr. Spock does advise that if the drive is so intense that the child fashions one out of a clothespin we shouldn't make an issue of it. He sees the ideal situation as all parents in the neighborhood agreeing to ban guns [Dr. Jerilyn Prior, "Violence, Childcare & Sexism: Dr. Spock Interviewed," *Win,* 21 February 1974, pp. 10-11].

Our own reflections at this point brought on guilt feelings regarding our older children. We thought they had been deprived because their upbringing was in an atmosphere of glorified aggressiveness. It seemed that we had bungled badly.

Our intentions for Mark, however, did not reckon with his potential. He turned into a robust storehouse of energy with a unique ability to grasp any situation. Neighborhood friends and TV had their effect, so soon he was galloping through the house "plugging" desperados right and left with varied shaped pieces of wood that were conjured up in his imagination to be blued steel six-shooters with the lightest of hair triggers. On those occasions when he became annoyed with us he would knowingly point a finger and emit a loud "BAM." The climax came when our oldest son gave him a two-gun set for Christmas. We couldn't miss the gleam in his eye when he saw it and we could visualize the outcome many years hence if some not-so-well-meaning friend should entice him with a real weapon. It was very plain that things were not working out as we planned and some serious rethinking was in order.

Taking a closer look at our grown sons, we found two of them had not used their rifles in years. They had satisfied themselves during their childhood. Our eldest likes to hunt but is scrupulously careful with firearms. All three understand guns and consequently are not enticed by some imagined mystique. Our daughters never did have a real interest in guns except when we used to take them out target shooting. They probably never think about such weapons. Why had we been worried that we had failed to teach our children healthy values in this respect? We have made mistakes but raising violent children was not one of them. They always knew that they were loved and that is what really counts.

So we faced a decision regarding Mark. Should we continue the new method which so far appeared ineffective, or should we revert to practices which had been successful with us in spite of differing advice from noted people in the field? Or is there another way that uses the best points of both methods? One thing we had learned well in our years of child raising is that if you prohibit something it becomes a powerful attraction. The prominent psychologist Rollo May explains:

> The normal development of an infant requires the love and care of the parent along with his own capacity to

explore and increase his sense of mastery day by day. . . .
[Anthony] Storr does not believe that reading Grimms
Fairy Tales and playing cops and robbers and war
games is harmful for children. The child has no
difficulty separating fantasy from reality, and he needs
to work out his aggressive tendencies in fantasy if they
are not to be acted out in reality. Quoting [D.W.]
Winnicott. . . "If Society is in danger, it is not because of
man's aggressiveness but because of the repression of
personal aggression in individuals." Storr goes on to
propose that parents who are anxious that their
children not turn into war mongers may, by proscribing
war games and the like, be cultivating just the opposite.
They "are more likely to create the very type of
personality which they are concerned to avoid." For the
child needs all the aggressive potential he can get to
protect and assert his growing individuality. (Rollo May,
Power and Innocence [New York: W.W. Norton & Co.,
1972] pp. 125-126.)

It seemed to us that our children had to work their
violence out at an early age or else they would do it later.
We decided to let Mark play with toy guns and he
acquired quite a collection. We express our opinion that
guns should be used only for target shooting although he
sees them used differently on TV and sometimes
pretends to do so himself. Once we asked him if he
thought that the best solution was to kill off his enemies.
"It's just make believe," he replied. "I wouldn't really do
that."

The reality of the situation goes deeper than just
fantasy. Mark enjoys a loving relationship with us and he
recognizes that we respect his right to make some
decisions, although he knows we do not always agree.
Allowing him to make choices commensurate with his age
stimulates reasoning and develops responsibility.

Dr. Spock's advice does, to some extent, open the door
to talking things out, but beyond that it tends to impress
our ideas upon children without giving them the freedom
to experiment and learn. This has been a failing in child
raising for many years and has often forced children to
adopt society's norms rather than develop their own
values. That impressed ethic may not be personally

accepted which, in itself, is a dangerous source of interior conflict. In addition, such an arrangement with neighbors—as Dr. Spock recommends—would create an unreal environment and the subsequent shock when real life situations are encountered might easily spark rejection of many learned values. This again opens the door for violence.

As a boy Bob admits having an uncanny craving for a sidearm and without his toy six-shooter he felt naked. Often he was careless where he left it and the replacement rate was high. After many warnings his parents finally refused to buy any more "fowlin' pieces" until he could take better care of them. In desperation he searched all over until, in a barnyard puddle of water and horse manure, he found a dirty, smelly piece of wood which appeared in his fantasies as a beautiful revolver. He had always placed his "hardware" under his pillow at night where it would be readily available in case of emergency, and that's exactly where this obnoxious object went. All through the next day it was carefully wedged into a holster except for frequent, lightning-like withdrawals when his reputation had to be defended against mythical assailants. Bob was resigned to the fact that he'd have to make do with that piece of wood for some time.

That evening Bob and his parents drove to town where he waited with his mom in the Model-A Ford while his dad went into Montgomery Ward's to buy some "necessities." The next morning his happiness was unbounded when he found a shiny new replica of Samuel Colt's famed .44 under his pillow.

Today it is not so much the toy pistol that remains in Bob's memory as his parent's understanding when they saw how much he desired that toy. This incident took place during the early 1930s and he now realizes that refusing to continually replace his lost weapons was also tied to their economic straits—which lends even greater warmth to their generosity. These little acts of love sometimes take years to reach full realization in our consciousness but their effect is manifold when they do.

If we have come to appreciate the beauty of nonviolence it is not because guns were kept out of reach as we grew up but because we experienced love. Rollo May pointed out that the need for love and care being unmet is the real cause of violence in a personality whereas the blocking of aggression tends to make a person dependent:

> In origin the infant shows his power and aggression always in conjunction with its opposite—i.e., with his need to be dependent and to be nourished. . . If his aggressiveness is blocked, as is often the case with suburban middle-class children, he will tend to remain forever dependent. Or if his need for love and care is unmet, he may well become destructively aggressive and spend his life wreaking revenge upon the world— as is sometimes the case with children brought up in the slums. Or if he has no boundaries, nothing against which to test his strength, no opposition in the firmness of parents, he may turn his aggression against himself in nail-biting and self-recrimination or senseless anger against anyone who happens to come along (*Power And Innocence*, op cit, p. 124).

This is a crucial point to understand in order for a parent to successfully guide children through their formative years. We blundered into the right way to release tension in our children although there are many other aspects in which we could have improved. It is much better to enter this joyous responsibility with a clear understanding of where we want to go and the best way to get there.

We need to inject a word of caution about real guns. Working out frustrations in fantasy with toy weapons is one thing but when children are old enough to want a real one—whether a B-B gun or firearm—a new complexity arises. That real weapon is dangerous! Ignorance of firearm safety can be disastrous. Bob's father was an expert with guns and was able to guide him through without mishap. Some of his ability rubbed off onto Bob—although he is a terrible marksman he is a stickler for safety. We have seen many tragedies resulting from children being turned loose with guns; consequently we lean toward gun control laws not only because we believe they are likely to reduce crime but also because appropriate legislation will reduce the number of accidents caused by firearms entering the hands of inexperienced people.

On the other hand, when handled safely, rifles can be just as recreational as archery or golf. (We would exclude pistols as recreational items because of the ease they can be concealed and their association with crime, although some would disagree on this point.) Our family will continue to enjoy target practice on future outings so the children can satisfy some of their curiosity under guidance and at the same time learn safety precautions that may someday save a life.

Nevertheless, we haven't slipped back completely into the old methods. One change from former practice is that we now control TV because we feel that what enters our home and influences our children should be decided by us. Sometimes a "shoot 'em up" feature sneaks in, but even then we find that the subsequent discussion provides fruitful dialogue. Helpful as that may be, we still feel it is best not to expose young children to those types of programs unnecessarily—they find out about violence soon enough as it is.

The California Commission on Crime Control and Violence Prevention reported that children "spent more time watching television than any other single activity. Even children at the lower end of the TV use spectrum— 2.5 hours of viewing per day—will have spent more time in front of a television set by the time they are 18 years of age than in the classroom." The report calculates that by the age of 18 the average person has witnessed 18,000 murders and points out that 60 percent of prime time television story programs contain violent solutions to conflict situations. Even cartoons contain considerable violence and the Commission noted one Saturday morning cartoon which contained 64 acts of violence in an hour.

No wonder a May 1982 Gallup Poll revealed that 66 percent of Americans see a link between TV and real world violence. A ban on televising violent programs before 10:00 PM was endorsed by 67 percent of the public. Instead there seems to be an upswing in prime time television violence—from five violent acts per hour in December 1980 to almost seven by May 1981, a 40 percent increase in only five months. Furthermore, since commercial films are more graphically violent in their content than made-for-television programs, the commission expects the amount and severity of violence viewed at home to increase as the home video market expands.

Besides desensitizing children to violent behavior in their everyday world, TV violence also distorts their perception of others and the world in general. Antagonistic reactions are stimulated as well as unrealistic fear of crime and violence. Furthermore, as research findings have shown, watching TV violence does not provide an outlet for personal frustrations, rather it increases the likelihood of children using violence against their foes as well as increasing the severity of violence used. In short, depiction of violence on TV teaches children that it is an appropriate response to frustration and provides the "how to" of certain violent behavior. This should be heavy food-for-thought for parents.

Another difference from our former practice with our children is that corporal punishment is now out in our book. Spanking and slapping can no longer be justified. Children learn from the example we parents show and corporal punishment exhibits violence. Although it may obtain the instantaneous result we want at the time, at least outwardly, it seldom has any beneficial lasting effect.

We parents need the patience to practice methods which are more effective over the long haul but may require months or even years to show fruition. We should also be aware that the incidents which we view as calling for punishment are often signs that the child needs loving firmness. We then have the choice of withholding that love, which is in itself a form of violence, or turning our passions to a caring response. In our social system of winners and losers, punishments are recognition for being bad and rewards are recognition for being good. Only love is recognition for just being. It is a happy fact that in childhood memories—the only really lasting influence that we parents can hope for—the more positive pleasant experiences usually predominate.

When immersed in a caring, nurturing environment, the playing of cops and robbers can scarcely be considered a threat to the child's nature. On the contrary, such activity provides a means of working off tensions and stimulating a feeling of power which is so important to self-esteem. Mark found his own way of using toy pistols—his plea of "Will you shoot darts with me?" was his way of letting me know he wanted companionship. A lot of parental weaknesses and blundering can be submerged by a little bit of love.

6

Peer Groups and the Wider Community

It is not rebellion itself which is noble
but the demands it makes upon us.
—*Albert Camus*
La Peste (1947)

When Mary was in her teens she started out with the usual objections to hand-me-down clothes. Being our fourth daughter she received plenty of them. One day Bob remarked that it was dumb to buy new merchandise when we could get good clothing a lot cheaper. This particular advantage of secondhand shopping appealed to Mary because it allowed her to stretch her clothes budget farther. Soon she and her friends, some from rather prosperous families, were making the rounds of thrift shops and Salvation Army stores.

More than saving money was involved when we urged Mary to be less of a consumer. Under today's practice of large businesses exploiting poor countries to provide commodities, living simply is integral to a nonviolent lifestyle. Mary was more receptive to these values than some of our children.

It is during these adolescent years that children begin to question their parents' values. At this age they are constantly fluctuating between the comfort of being dependent and the yearning for self-determination, feeling the urge to strike out on their own but at the same time being timid about leaving the security and guidance of mom and dad. This is a normal and healthy process of growing up. Parents should welcome it and not feel offended by the questioning, as so many fathers and mothers tend to do. Instead of being concerned about our own prestige, we as parents need to be particularly sensitive to our children's feelings because they are going through turmoil—torn between the demands and fun seeking of their peers and the advice of their parents.

During this crucial time of adolescence youngsters are testing parental values against what they hear from friends to develop their own priorities. It is also a time when as parents we are called upon to rethink our values and make revisions as necessary to put our priorities in line with our beliefs. Many of the actions and words of our children during these stressful years do not necessarily indicate the values they will eventually form. But how we parents handle situations during this delicate period will have a direct influence on those emerging values.

Since our family lives in a middle income neighborhood, our children do not come in frequent contact with poor and oppressed families. On the other hand, because of our commitment to a simple life-style we do much of our clothes shopping at second-hand stores where fashions are a little behind. By making use of such articles we help to cut down the drain on our resources while allowing us to have adequate clothing, but also this allows us to live on a lesser income so we do not have to be a slave to a job in order to meet our needs. There are, of course, still more advantages to reducing consumption of goods and living on less income.

Since the used clothes we purchase do not keep up with the latest styles, they fall short of meeting the criteria for elite approval and there are strong pressures put on our children to keep up with their well-dressed peers. Our three children still living at home—Diane, Nancy and Mark—have part-time jobs. Their pay is their own money and we let them spend it pretty much as they choose. Some of it, naturally, goes for new clothes. Although we would not buy some of the new garments they do, we believe children their age should be making their own decisions regarding money earned and try not to force our values on them, although they cannot help but be affected by their sharing in our simple life-style. Nevertheless, when the youngsters see that we respect their feelings they, in turn, become more receptive to ours. That leads to paying closer attention to our example as they form their own value structures.

Aside from allowing our teenagers to spend their money as they wish, we are still in somewhat of a quandary as to how closely we should control the occasions which influence their desire to spend. When the girls ask to go to a department store, Bob tends to ask if they have something specific in mind to purchase. If they just want to look around with their friends he tries to discourage the idea on the basis that it becomes too tempting to be consumers amid a world of starving people.

Janet, on the other hand, recalls looking through the mail order catalogs and picking out a whole new wardrobe when she was Diane's and Nancy's age since stores were too far away to go window shopping and, besides, she knew there wasn't enough money to buy anything. Janet is not convinced that this made her an unthinking consumer but it did allow her to work out her desire for new things in fantasy. She feels that window shopping can do the same thing for our daughters and if we do not make them feel guilty about it they will be more apt to learn from our attitude and example. Of course we do not allow spending beyond their budget or charging merchandise.

Our daily activities are different than the average people in our neighborhood. We do not spend most of our time working to support a high standard of living, which gives us more time to work for peace and justice. But our simple life-style does put an added burden on our adolescents. During the teen years it is much harder to cope if your parents are "different." They are easily embarrassed over their parents anyway and this aggravates the situation. But with loving understanding and guidance, these teens can be shown how to turn embarrassment into a good example. We must remain confident in the fact that, in the long run, the home environment has more influence than peers and school combined. Keeping that in mind, we need not become too anxious but can patiently counsel and persuade our children to recognize the truth as it exists in the world today. Through loving patience we can turn embarrassment into pride and eventually leadership.

Our adolescent children have joined us in many nonviolent demonstrations. They understand that we participate in these activities because of sincere convictions and that has a tremendous influence on them. But accepting our invitation to participate with us is a free choice they make. They know they do not have to if they choose not to. In a few well planned instances these activities have led to our being arrested. Diane once told us that at first it was hard for her to tell her friends that her parents had spent time in jail for citizen intervention—a term which more adequately describes what some people call civil disobedience. When a citizen takes action to obey a higher law—constitutional ànd international law—or to prevent a great harm, that action is legally justified by the principle of necessity and is not disobedient. Unfortunately many courts do not recognize this constitutionally protected right of due process when nuclear war or government policy are involved. Diane remembers how she was bothered when a friend called our action "stupid." Now she proudly tells us it no longer disturbs her because she understands the urgency of alerting people to the danger of nuclear weapons.

And as Mary involved her friends in shopping at secondhand stores, she showed strength and influenced her peers. That required courage because it is not easy to take a stand in the face of possible ridicule, especially when the pressure to conform is so great. In addition, spending money in these places helps small business ventures and charitable organizations rather than patronizing large and exploitative corporations.

Schools tend to reinforce, if not instill, the attitude of conformity and unquestioning acceptance. Nowhere is this clearer than in terms of patriotism. Democracy is subtly impressed upon the students as preservation of the status quo with decision making relegated to the experts. Participatory democracy involving creative and often extensive change is not taught except by a few insightful teachers. By and large schools tend to uphold the general attitude that attempts to change our country are subversive and unacceptable to loyal Americans.

In school the kids are exposed to history books which portray only the glamorous side of our nation's past so they do not learn such controversial information as the takeover of lands from the Native American Indians or the massacre at Wounded Knee—or the breaking of treaties with them to give the privileged access to gold and then oil and, today, uranium. American presidents are portrayed as respectable leaders instead of the slave-owning and corrupt individuals that many of them were.

History books also accentuate the glories of war, as do museums and other institutions. This is not to imply that schools are all a cover-up of our violent past and exploitative present. One must recognize many educators with deeper insight who are trying hard to balance the education of the students entrusted to their classrooms. Nevertheless, even under the guidance of such well-intentioned teachers, it is hard for children—even secondary school aged—to understand what is going on in this country without help at home. In a sheltered environment these young people just cannot comprehend the part that corporations play in our economy and the effects of our foreign policy on Third World countries. Very few school age youth realize that the United States only comprises six percent of the global population but consumes 40 percent of the world's resources and possesses 50 percent of the wealth.

How can we parents balance this lopsided education which idolizes violence and teaches children to "look out for Number One"? We do not pretend to have the complete answer but we are convinced that the schools will change only after enough parental attitudes change. As parents we should remain acutely aware that the total education of our children is our personal responsibility even though we have allowed the state to legislate what education shall be. Under today's circumstances, meaningful communication with our children is more necessary than ever. We cannot merely deride what the children are learning or they will sympathize with the object of our attack. But neither should parents be a rubber stamp for a teacher who upholds what is deficient in our educational system. When it has been definitely ascertained that learning is on the wrong track something has to be done to provide children with information so they can approach the truth through their own processes. There is no prescribed formula for accomplishing this and it takes a lot of awareness, ingenuity and thinking on the parents' part. The approach will differ with every child. Perhaps the key is awareness.

Our daughter Mary was a senior in high school during the 1976 presidential election and her civics class was studying the candidates. A good friend of ours, the late Frederick Douglas Kirkpatrick, managed to get on the ballot as a presidential candidate in a few states. Brother Kirk, as he was called, was a black man—the son of Louisiana sharecroppers who had suffered terribly as a victim of racism and had pledged his life to combat oppression of the poor. At first he used violent methods, but under the influence of Martin Luther King, Jr. he traded his gun for a guitar and became a troubadour for justice. As he put it, "Wherever people are poor or oppressed or hungry, there I am with my political songs and music to unmask that injustice."

Brother Kirk came to California that year to support the anti-Trident missile campaign. We became responsible for arranging his appearances at various university, church and civic groups and Mary asked if he would speak to her civics class as a presidential candidate. He agreed. Mary then proposed to her teacher the idea of having a real candidate speak to her class, who in turn took it up with the principal. Knowing that Mary liked to rock the boat, the principal tried to discourage the idea by requiring that all presidential candidates have equal time. Mary and her friends were not so easily put off and telephoned the campaign offices. The Democrats could not make it, but the Republicans agreed to send a speaker. Teacher and principal had to accept.

At the class meeting Brother Kirk's straightforward facts, his songs and his sincerity far overshadowed the pat line of the professional politician—even high school students could see through under those circumstances. The debate was a simple illustration of how the plain truth outshines rationalized propaganda if the truth is allowed to be heard. The teacher, as well as the dean of students who monitored the class, admitted that they were impressed.

More to the point, Mary's arrangement for her civics class is a poignant example of how students and home can improve formalized class education. Unfortunately, just as too many working people plan their living around a job and subjugate family plans to the boss' demands, too many parents look to the schools as the primary source of learning. Schools, of course, reinforce that notion and attendance is mandatory. Sickness is recognized as the only excused absence according to the rules which allocate finances from the state on the basis of attendance. Consequently, absences are discouraged because if the average head count goes down, so does the budget.

This preempts parental discretion on what takes priority over attending school. Nevertheless, on special occasions such as when we are going out of town or one of the kids has the opportunity to accompany one of us on a trip, we allow them to miss school and truthfully explain the reason. The children agree to make up work missed and these occasions are not so frequent that they get behind. Some experiences are more important than school; whether that be another form of learning, a special way for the family to have fun together, or a time to be alone with one parent. It is also refreshing for both children and parents to break from the stilted decision making driven by economics. It is not wise for this to happen too often, however.

One such occasion arose when Bob and several others were going on trial for a citizen intervention action to stop construction of the Trident missile at Lockheed. They would be representing themselves and would be giving facts to the jury regarding the necessity to trespass. We thought it would be educational for Diane and Nancy, then in junior high school, to observe a political trial of this nature so we allowed them to miss school. We called them our "little court watchers." Most of the testimony was completed in two days so we thought it better for them to return to school for the third. Diane was disappointed and begged to go to the last day of the trial. We said we would think about it and let her know in the morning. That night when we went to bed Bob found a note on his desk from Diane.

Read This

Dad,

   I am still interested in being a courtwatcher
tomorrow. I would appreciate it if I could go tomorrow.
I especially want to go if you are pretty sure you will
win the case.

   I have got my school work all planned out, so I could
get all caught up Monday night. I'm already ahead in
half of my classes anyway.

   Since I have a dentist appointment at 2:30 I can leave
at 1:30 and catch a bus. They have buses stop every 10
min. I know the route and I'll have plenty of time to get
to the dentist.

   I have everything all planned out, you can ask me all
about it tomorrow.

                    Love Always,
                    Diane, May 20, 1979

In the face of such enthusiasm and planning we could
hardly refuse her request. This enlightenment is undoubtedly why she now sees that going to jail in an effort
to end the arms race is a proper thing for a Christian to
do.

   One of Diane's friends got in trouble for cutting too
many classes. We were a little anxious about what kind of
influence that would have on Diane but when we
brought the subject up she said she was not interested in
skipping classes for such small pleasures. She would
rather have good attendance and keep up with her
studies so she could miss school when something important comes along. This development of responsibility was
a welcome bonus which we hadn't anticipated.

   It is easier to develop responsibility in children when
there is a community of parents, so to speak, to share
with. When our older children were living at home our
friends had children about the same age as ours. That is
no longer true and we hardly know the parents of
Diane's, Nancy's and Mark's friends because our interests are so different. Mark has brought us into contact
with other parents through his interest in soccer and Cub
Scouts, but until recently we have not had any deep

philosophical discussions with them because our contacts have been on a more superficial level. Lately, we have made a special effort to become better acquainted and that has been successful. Nevertheless, it has been difficult for the children because their activities have been curtailed because of a difference in values.

We have always tried to stay in touch with parents of our children's closest friends, however. Even if we don't know the parents well, we still require that they be present when our children visit. We do not allow visiting at either the friend's house or our house unless either the mother or father is home. Because of this rule we try to find out as much as possible about other parents— what they will allow and what they won't. At some homes our children were not allowed to stay overnight because the rules, or lack of rules, conflict with our ideas of what is safe and what is not.

For instance, our children are not allowed to roam the streets after dark and we are strict on that point. We also do not believe in unlimited television viewing. To some this may seem overprotective but we feel the limits must be real and practical. Once set, those limits should be consistently enforced although in an atmosphere which makes the youngsters know they are loved. Of course they should be allowed freedom to experiment within those limits and then the limits widened as the youngsters accept responsibility and show a readiness to set their own realistic bounds. Too rigid limitation can foster dependency, but excessive leniency breeds irresponsibility and lack of consideration for others.

Actually, there are times when children want to be told no. Sometimes they will ask permission to do something just to see if we care enough about them to refuse. "Can I go to a beach party with boys and girls unchaperoned Saturday night?" asked one of the girls at the time she was 13. Our answer was an unequivocal NO! Years later she told us that she did not really want to go but just wanted to see what we would say. The point is that teenagers do not always desire what they ask for. Sometimes they lack the courage to refuse their friends and it is easier to put the blame on mom and dad. Other times they just want to know that we care enough to protect them.

Usually it is not even necessary to refuse a request. Sometimes we will say we do not feel good about it but will think it over. It seems that at least half the time the youngster will come back later and say never mind because other plans have been made, or the child will present a more acceptable alternative. This techniques encourages them to think things through and make good decisions.

At other times we still have to say no after thinking it over. Nevertheless, it is better to take the matter under consideration than to give a hasty answer. If the denial appears to be an offhand decision, youngsters may feel resentful, thinking their request was not adequately considered. We try to avoid quick answers, especially if they would be negative. Refusals are much better received when it is known the matter has been given thought.

In the debate between permissiveness and over-protectiveness we have found that letting children have their every desire does not communicate that we care for them. But it is often easier to grant a request than to face the sulking, arguments or other forms of expressed displeasure which often follow a refusal. It makes a lot of difference how it is done, but when something needs to be refused it should be refused, as in the example of our not allowing our children to roam around at night. There are conditions which warrant exceptions, but one reason for the rule is the safety of the children. Some parents feel that we are being too protective, but there is still another reason for not allowing this.

We feel one of the limits children should have is adequate supervision which, as with other limits, can be relaxed as they accept responsibility for their own bounds. Although supervision does not necessarily mean constant adult attention, it does entail encouraging youngsters to act with a purpose. The tendency today is for young people to drift aimlessly with the crowd which is also drifting aimlessly. This often leads to mischief. Lack of purpose is also manifested in excessive TV watching but it can also take more serious forms such as seeking excitement from drugs, gangs and other forms of undesirable behavior.

In Santa Clara County where we live there is a lot of trouble with cruising—where many youngsters with cars cruise up and down a main thoroughfare. This goes on for hours after dark, usually on weekends. It happens more consistently in some neighborhoods but, as much as residents would like to prevent it, the larger and regularly scheduled rallies take place in the more elite sections of town. This activity reflects boredom and the lack of direction on the part of youth, and has led to gangs congregating in shopping center parking lots for immoral and destructive behavior. Vandalism, broken windows, graffiti and general littering are all part of the picture, for the seeming anonymity of the crowd leads young people to all sorts of malicious behavior. These things don't just happen, they start much earlier in life and are chiefly offshoots from poor supervision and lack of parental direction.

A poor sense of direction also leads to other major problems such as vandalism on public property, schools and parks. The disruptiveness of children in schools has led to tighter discipline and barrages of rules and regulations. Then when children grow up the anonymity they have experienced creates a mass society in which people become insensitive to the needs and feelings of others and apathetic toward violence and injustice. Their poor sense of direction creates a loss in self-confidence as youth follow the crowd and fail to exercise the thinking required of a good leader. These conditions can inevitably be traced to poor guidance and lack of purpose during childhood years. Such unwanted behavior can be avoided if parents show abundant love and set definite but fair limits.

We have found that it is important to set time aside each day when youngsters can share the events of the day—a time to ask questions or maybe just be silly with us. Laughing at special TV programs together, doing exercises together and playing catch together are means of showing attention and allowing opportunities for communication. Sometimes the children tend to share more with us spontaneously, when they sense our availability rather than at a set time. At other times they will ask one of us to take them somewhere alone so they can have our full attention—to be the "only child" or discuss something special. Occasionally we will initiate the encounter by asking them to stop at a coffee shop for a cup of chocolate so we can have that special time alone. Ingenuity can turn up many ways to guide young lives with attention and love. They are made possible when a family communicates.

Keeping the lines of communication open among parents and children is one of the most important, if not the most important, part of child raising. It starts in infancy, continuing through the grade school years and into adolescence, changing form and technique all the time. Communication actually goes on for the remainder of our lives but is probably the most difficult when children are in their teens.

During their teen years it is vital that we communicate with respect—actually communicating respect so they can see it. This means talking to them as if they were adults but not necessarily expecting an adult response. Treating them as equals builds a good self-image because they see themselves as capable of talking on the adult level and that image is critical at this stage of life. Teenagers need to know they are good, capable, lovable, dependable and all the other things which foster self-esteem. For us to let them know these things requires sincere communication so they realize we appreciate those character traits when we see them. The teen years are extremely difficult years—this crossing the line from childhood to adult-hood—and teenagers need all the support and confidence we can give them. They need to be able to make mistakes and accept the consequences while at the same time learning from those mistakes. It is part of helping them fail successfully.

Once on a family camping trip, one of our teen girls insisted she did not need to take along a pair of tennis shoes and that her zoris were sufficient. It turned out that she was pretty cold and miserable. Janet was tempted to loan her a pair of shoes but decided it would be better to let her accept the consequences rather than become dependent on someone for rescue. Had she been offered a pair of shoes it would have magnified her misjudgment and diminished her self-image. Instead, she learned something because she is now quite attentive to taking proper clothes and footwear.

Example is probably the most powerful medium of communication. When we cheat and lie and use bad language we are telling our children that we condone such behavior, regardless of how strongly we say the opposite. In addition, the double standard causes our children to lose respect for us and, ultimately, themselves. Living up to high but attainable goals is the surest way of letting children know they are good and that good is expected from them—that they are the kind of people who do good.

Communication consumes time. Sometimes we just have to take that time at the most inopportune moment. Children need to know they are top priority. If, on the other hand, communication has not been good in the family it is a challenge to improve it. We know that we could all stand improvement. We could all be more ready to communicate and more sincere when we do communicate. When we lose our patience and later feel sorry, it is important to let them know we are sorry. They understand well and they are good at apologizing, too.

Communication, love, caring, direction of purpose, guidance, reasonable limits and failing successfully are key factors in raising children from cradle to adulthood. As their environment expands to where they are influenced more and more from outside the home, this base of love and caring and communication must be maintained—even intensified—to keep the children on the right track and feeling good about themselves. The responsibilities are great but so is the fulfillment. As parents we receive many bonuses, such as the Valentine's Day message Mary composed:

Mom and Dad,

Valentine's Day to me is a day to express the love I have for someone special, like you. But it is hard for me to show you that I love and care for you every minute of the day. All I can do is try my best. I can't tell you how much you mean to me and how much I want to raise my kids like you are doing. Through the little ones

I can see what beautiful parents you are. I love you very much and always will, so remember that please. I love you.

XO XO XO	Love always,
XO XO XO	Mary
XO XO XO	P.S. Happy Valentine's Day

7

Values and Attitudes

What gives life its value you can find—and lose.
But never possess. This holds good above all for
"the Truth about life."
                                    —*Dag Hammarskjold*
                                    Markings

We pushed our older children very hard to get them
through the grades in school. At that time we believed in
competing vigorously, but fairly, to establish ourselves in
a comfortable position. We viewed such attainment as a
major goal. We also had a "Christian concern" for less
fortunate people in poorer countries, but at the same
time thanked God for our good fortune to be born in
America. Making the grade in school consequently was a
big thing and we set aside certain times each day for the
kids to sit down and study. How much they actually
accomplished under these circumstances is debatable but,
apply themselves or not, they had to put in the time.

We were also impressed in those early years with the
resourceful manner in which friends of ours managed to
start their daughter in school at an early age. According
to California law she lacked a few weeks of being old
enough for the first grade. Consequently, her mother
rented a cabin on the east shore of Lake Tahoe and
enrolled the girl in a Nevada school where the age
requirement was more flexible. After a few weeks the
daughter was then transferred to a California school
near her home. We hailed this accomplishment as a
triumph over bureaucratic red tape and as giving the girl
an early start in life. Although we didn't fully comprehend it at the time, our attitude was in full accord with
the society's pressure to achieve worldly success.

It became clear to us in the intervening years that our society is a violent society. Furthermore, excessive pressure to succeed is a form of craving which leads to a violent attitude. When we practice this in the family we are introducing potential violence. Nonviolence, also, is closely related to values and attitudes for it stems from an attitude to uphold the value of life and dignity for all people. It grows from within the person and is a manifestation of the character of that person. When our desire to become nonviolent waxes strong, we find ourselves eschewing the use of violence, either overt or subtle, to attain our goals. Achieving a nonviolent personality is a continuous struggle to recognize violent emotions so they can be dealt with in a constructive manner—that is, providing an outlet for those emotions which are not harmful and, hopefully, beneficial. As the emotional experience of nonviolence matures, love and compassion begin to shine through the facade of strength and respectability. As nonviolence integrates into our personality we become more anxious to replace the evil of violence with a more palatable social order.

At one time we likened the struggle for interior nonviolence to transcending basic instinct. Now we are not sure that is a good analogy. The instinct of self-preservation is very strong, true, but a stronger instinct is preservation of the species. It is not uncommon for animals to sacrifice themselves to save their pack or herd. Although this is instinctual behavior, it does put the collective well-being above individual safety. When this behavior is extended to human beings as an attitude, due to their consciousness and reasoning ability, it is only natural that a loving and caring personality will result. Using this line of reasoning, we can conclude that nonviolence is just as much a natural tendency as violence is ascribed to be. It is probably even more natural because it derives from the stronger instinct. That being true, nonviolence is not an unattainable dream but is a realistic goal for an individual and also for a society of people. When it is achieved at the social level it will introduce a whole new pattern of living and could be the beginning of real civilization.

Why then is violence so prevalent in our society? We

might theorize that because humanity is rational we can see the personal satisfaction of comfort and gain. We then rationalize that comfort is pleasant so we seek more of it. Soon our comfort becomes an overriding priority and begins to usurp the supply of resources and the rights of others. Conflict sets in and seeking comfort and gain becomes a contest of strength. We arm ourselves and pass laws to protect our property and preserve our possessions. We build fences, buy watch dogs, install burglar alarms. On the national scale we build armies and weapons to protect our "interests." Our desire for comfort and gain soon manifests itself in the violence of a massive arms race.

Weapons competition is violent in more ways than the capacity of those weapons if they are ever unleashed. We do not have to wait for the bombs to fall before the violence begins. As cumulative efforts seek military strength, and our individual efforts personal gain, the misappropriation of resources deprives the masses of people their just share. This resultant violence directed against their natural right to a just life causes them to become desperate and strike back. They steal and cheat and wreak vengeance on a society where the rich are strong and being poor is a disgrace. Respect deteriorates on both sides of the economic gap. We build jails to lock up thieves and pass laws to execute murderers. Violence gains momentum as we become inured to it and, in fact, justify it. Greed and selfishness grow as social institutions fall apart. Not the least of these institutions are marriage and family.

On the global level the pattern is similar. We are a prosperous nation but many of our neighbors to the south are not. Driven by destitution, people from these countries migrate north to work in America's bountiful fields and orchards. They become fugitives in a hostile land because their presence is illegal. Legality aside, they are recruited in their own country, enticed across the border, and then exploited through low wages and poor working conditions. As long as they do not complain, they have a job of sorts. As soon as they voice discontent they are reported to the US Immigration and Naturalization Service and deported. The pattern goes on and on with many more examples of transnational exploitation by big business—even to the point of forging US foreign policy which supports dictators who repress their own people to create a favorable climate for US investment.

As wealth is acquired, avarice sets in to accumulate more wealth. The dollar becomes the primary measure of value and success, and our attitude toward all decisions becomes economically oriented. Other important values fade as material goods and property ownership suffocate any reverence for life and any compassion toward human needs. We grow as hard and cold as the dollar which motivates us, viewing poor people as lazy—as parasites who drain our wealth with welfare checks and social programs. The desperate are locked up where they cannot threaten our possessions rather than being rehabilitated by seeking the cause and cure for their antisocial behavior. The truth seems to be that we do not want to find that cause or cure because it would upset our profit making potential.

On the national level, patriotism is promoted. This concentration on our own well-being tends to isolate us from those suffering in poorer countries. Our leaders tell us we need a strong military to protect our national interests. Very few of us pause to reflect on what those national interests are—a high standard of living which consumes resources at an irreplaceable rate while exploiting the best land and cheapest labor available in Third World countries. All of this is done to enhance our life-style. Even fewer of us question the credibility of those leaders who have been put in office through the money and influence of large corporations—whose stockholders and executives are getting inordinately rich on defense contracts, transnational operations, foreign arms sales and hawking the myriads of gadgets to an overconsuming public.

It seems that in America we are becoming more and more divided as either winners or losers. The winners get the jobs with the large incomes and have the opportunity to buy the most consumer goods. The losers populate the slums, perform the menial labor and fight the wars to protect the winners' interests. Competition is vigorous as people seek to enhance their own interests without being too concerned about those who do not have the opportunity to succeed.

Unfortunately, when we scrutinize this we realize that the screening process for winners and losers is our educational system. Competition starts in the early grades and continues on into high school and college. The mark of a successful competitor is a high grade point average which is a measure of that student's worth to the industrialized, corporate society. This was dramatically underscored in a 1972 remark by Glenn Dumke, then chancellor of the California State University and College System. He said, "The purpose of education is to teach people how to live in society. Our society is competitive and nasty, and grades help people learn how to be competitive and nasty" (Cited in December 1975 brochure mailed to constituents by John Vasconcellos, Assembly-man for the 23rd District, California).

Throughout the primary and intermediate grades our youngsters are heavily indoctrinated in how to become competitive and nasty. They receive a skewed picture of American history, the glorification of the military and exercises in patriotism. Competition is also fostered through athletic programs which, ostensibly, are for physical education and to learn fair play. In practice they contribute heavily to aggressive personality traits.

In high school the grading system is even more significant because it screens those who will be allowed to enter colleges and universities. Then conditions intensify in advanced education. College administrators generally do not ask what students want to learn or how they want to learn it. Instead, students are presented with a choice of several fully outlined curricula which perpetuate outworn practices in a spirit of academic tradition. Prejudices and mistakes are passed from the previous generation to the next while attempts at fresh approaches are squelched.

The university student's achievement is then measured by the so-called bell curve grading system which assumes that each classroom contains the normal distribution of intelligence. Erroneous as that may be, when it is combined with psychological resistance to testing, the inability of some to express their knowledge in a pre-scribed form, cultural barriers and other handicaps, this system of grading is not representative. It is effective, nonetheless, in skimming off the individuals who will fit best into the highly competitive industrial atmosphere. For the predestined failures, by present standards, the results are an increased feeling of insecurity and inferiority. Rather than seeking to overcome the students' obstacles to learning, the educational system simply weeds them out.

Frustration leads these losers to seek other avenues of fulfillment. Military recruiters on high school and college campuses conduct intensive public relations campaigns which appeal to shattered egos, but totally misrepresent life in the armed forces. To impressionable youth, however, this often appears as an opportunity to offset academic incapability and before they have a chance to experience life they are locked into military adventurism.

This concept of heroism and patriotism received a big boost during World War II. Perhaps there was no way then to avoid becoming involved when the major powers were in open aggression, but applying today the "My Country, Right or Wrong" mentality to Third World people resisting oppression is fallacious logic. This is especially true when it is our country that is supporting repressive dictatorships and corporate exploitation in those poorer countries. We cannot employ ancient remedies, which have never cured the basic ailment, to today's sickness. We would be wise to examine the symptoms and treat the cause. Unfortunately, most of our involvement in foreign affairs cannot stand close scrutiny and is thus too secret for us to know about. But our national effect on other societies is something each of us should understand better in order to meaningfully fulfill our vocations as parents. Failure to be informed is tantamount to driving a school bus blindfolded: it is going to mess up a lot of young lives.

For too long a time we have glorified war and violence. The concept of defending our vital interests has been overplayed. The most spectacular museum exhibits and monuments recall some military battle. This focus has perpetuated the "military solution" to international problems and has motivated young men to flaunt their muscles at every perceived chance to protect their home-land. One of our greatest scientists, Albert Einstein, who has published over 300 scientific papers and books, abhorred the glorification of war and militant nationalism. He said: "Our schoolbooks glorify war and hide its horrors. They inculcate nationalism and war in the veins of our children. I would teach peace rather than war. I would inculcate love rather than hate."

It is important that parents study facts to make germane decisions—even radical decisions—rather than cling to opinions held 30 or 40 years ago. Confronting the issues requires having a willingness to change our viewpoint when a new aspect of truth is perceived. This is scary because it could lead to changing our life-style. Most of us seem content to cling to old philosophies, no matter how faulty, to remain comfortable. Nevertheless, in this dynamic world growth must continue with all its pangs and pains. In the final analysis it may take deeper heroism to face up to the problems and work out solutions.

Our oldest son Cres encountered the draft before we had liberalized our outlook. We now believe that he wanted our help in facing up to the compulsory military service during the Indochina war—a specter that shadowed his planning for the future. Instead we gave him the patriotic line and shoved him ahead on his own. He didn't want to go to Vietnam to slaughter and possibly be slaughtered, so he made the best choice he could find and enlisted in the National Guard. We are proud that he did not give in to our advice and since that time our ideas have changed considerably. We now encourage our children to apply moral values to their decision-making. When Jim's time came, he applied for conscientious objector status which he obtained, as well as retroactive credit for a hospital job where he was already working. Danny did not even bother to register for a long time. When he later registered, the numbers of those to be called were already drawn and his birth date was not one of them. When selective service officials asked why he was so late he told them he just had not gotten around to it.

Exploitation of youth does not end if they survive military service. After Cres had completed his term of active duty he was beset by opportunists. The telephone's ring hailed a stream of calls from insurance salespeople vying to convert his government insurance policy. This, we learned, was a typical experience for the newly discharged. By the time we became aware of this practice, Cres had already yielded to the smooth sales pitch of an insurance agent we had at the time, without investigating all possibilities.

These same companies that compete so heavily to insure youthful lives put on another hat when it comes to automobiles. In this case youth are collectively condemned as unsafe drivers until they outgrow the fault of being young—something that now hangs on to some degree until they reach the age of 40. It is confirmation of the hold insurance companies have on government that they are able to practice such blatant class discrimination. Young people are forced to pay ridiculously high premiums to comply with financial responsibility laws which make life more abundant for insurance carriers.

When our daughter Jane was 22 she tried to insure her car with a different agent than our own. He told her she couldn't be insured because her parents were not his clients—this to a 22-year-old woman who had had no accidents during her six years of driving. When we challenged this statement he amended it to say: ". . . can't be insured at the regular rate." She would have to pay twice the normal premium.

Insurance companies defend their class-prejudice practices by producing statistics that show youth have more accidents. Agents, waving the latest National Safety Council report, shake a reproving finger at young people's youthfulness. If we were to examine the social picture more closely, we would likely find that one of the main reasons for those statistics is that our society impedes the development of reason and fosters irresponsibility. The macho mentality of our military oriented culture induces recklessness. The general conditioning in our environment promotes unsafe driving—one need only pay attention to television to understand that. Programs such as "Knight Rider" and "Mannix" are striking examples.

Automobile and petroleum industries also make their contribution to the poor driving records of impressionable young people. The "tiger in the tank" advertisement and its successors have been tested for veracity on the freeways with deadly results. Commercials featuring "cat grip tread" and "road hugging" suspensions are projected upon youthful minds amid a cacophony of squealing rubber and roaring engines. Impressionable youth tailor their driving habits accordingly. But first they need a car.

Slick automobile dealers wring their hands in anticipation as they see a gaping-mouthed youngster ogling the latest Detroit or Tokyo wonder. Autos serve basic transportation needs when used wisely, but muscle cars far surpass the limits of reasonableness and are incentives for trouble. Yet status buggies are perceived as a necessity by peer conscious young people who pay through the nose for a lot of tinsel and gingerbread. Unethical automobile and automobile accessory sales–persons surely know these facts but are apparently anxious to capitalize on them.

Observant parents can recognize how this fixation on maximizing profits in all areas is victimizing their youngsters as well as instilling a false sense of values on youth. The usual parental attitude seems to be that some cheating and swindling are expected and they proceed to teach their kids how to compete with it. But this everybody's-doing-it philosophy merely desensitizes the conscience while encouraging undesired behavior. The real emphasis should be on personal integrity and sticking to it.

This is all a rather condensed view of the forces which act upon us daily to uphold the dollar standard and numb our consciences. The family suffers because of this pressure and there is little community cooperation to raise responsible children. Although it is difficult for parents to buck this pattern, these malevolent forces can be opposed by persistence and stamina.

A few things we have tried in our family in this regard have been somewhat successful. First, we try to keep events in proper context. When children have a craving to buy something we ask them to wait a few days to see if they still feel as strongly about it. Sometimes their interest dwindles and they abandon the idea. At other times the desire persists and they buy the item. Nevertheless, this cooling off period helps them to handle the craving which advertisements stimulate.

When something is very disturbing or seems monumental, to keep our emotions in perspective another member of the family will ask, "Will this make any difference a hundred years from now?" Usually the answer to that question is negative and we can then begin to see that the anxiety or desire is not all that important. Where the answer to that question happens to be yes, we know we should do something. This is a very effective means of testing our perception of values and attitudes.

We have tried various experiments to help direct our family toward good values. Some values have changed drastically as in our attitude toward education. Whereas we used to view education and college as paramount and stressed with our older children that the only way for them to amount to anything in this world was to get a university degree, the concern about saving money for their higher education became a real anxiety for us. We nagged and harped and tried every means we could think of to keep them motivated. Some went to college for a while but none of them graduated until they were motivated on their own accord to do so.

Our attitude toward education is now quite changed. As regards the primary grades, we are not anxious to give the child an early start, feeling that the extra year of development at home does wonders in preparing the child for learning. More importantly, during that extra time the youngster develops a desire to learn, particularly in regard to reading. Children have a natural curiosity for stories and ours used to beg us to read at every opportunity. They were amazed at how those little marks and squiggles could convey such exciting information. Written words intrigue children as some form of secret code and they become anxious to decipher the mysteries. Mark used to say, "I just can't wait until I can read." That is a sign of fertile ground for learning.

This same principle applies when children have to struggle in later grades. Diane started first grade when she was barely six years old and was having trouble keeping up with the class. We considered keeping her back in third grade so she wouldn't be so overwhelmed and discussed this possibility with the teacher and principal. They disagreed, however, ostensibly because her grades weren't low enough. But the implication we sensed was that it would upset their schedule and the balance of pupils in each class.

Within a couple of months Diane had her tonsils removed, and she subsequently developed pneumonia. She missed a lot of school and got way behind. The teacher then agreed that Diane should be retained in the third grade—which turned out to be a real boost for her since her ability to excel in third grade work stimulated her confidence, and her enthusiasm for learning swelled. Now she is in college, obtaining good grades, and taking a keen interest in her studies which are no longer an ordeal for her.

In like manner our attitude toward higher education has also changed. We no longer feel that we owe our children higher education to the point of scrimping and saving to provide the best. When and if they see the value of further education, they will find a way of obtaining it while knowing we will help them as much as possible. They are then truly motivated and eventually appreciate what they have worked hard to obtain. As far as quality is concerned, we have found that local community colleges can often provide learning experiences and academic excellence on a par with prestigious universities. This is evidenced in such categories as field trips, class size and student-to-instructor relations.

This may seem like a cold attitude for parents to have but it has worked out best for us over the long haul. Our experience with children is that if they do not strongly desire and work for something, they do not value it. This seems to be human nature. There may be exceptions, of course, and each family will have to make careful and unbiased opinions in this regard.

Cres, our eldest, was pushed hard through college. We urged him to compete—to get in there and do well. He graduated from community college in the prescribed two years and then went to San Jose State University. Shortly after that he married, got tired of struggling for an education, and dropped out with less than a year to go. At the age of 31, after a decade of unfulfilling jobs, he decided to finish his degree so he could obtain the employment he desired in the field of natural science. But it was not until he was motivated that he really benefited from an education. Similar stories could be related about Janie and Jim, our second and third children.

Dan, our fourth child, never did relate to advanced education. He likes to work with his hands and aspired to an apprenticeship in the crafts. Now he is a good mechanic and manages his own furniture upholstery business. He doesn't create ulcers by status climbing. He keeps his business small, lives simply and finds time to enjoy some of the things he appreciates in life. Dan is a good citizen, conscientious about the feelings of others and spends time and money to benefit those less fortunate. Had we continued to push him through college it would have been frustrating for all of us. Instead, finally, we have encouraged him to pursue what he feels good about. Even so, he occasionally takes a college course in music or some other area of interest to him.

We have thus come to develop a cardinal rule: children should not be forced to replicate parental behavior. Some inhibitions and goals are required but basic values must be developed from models and experimentation. The parents' responsibility is to provide the proper model and safely guide the experimentation. Practicing poor values and saying something else is confusing and frustrating to the youngsters. As they get older they will normally adopt the values which we parents actually practice regardless of how much we vocalize the opposite.

Allowing the younger generation to arrive at their own value structure is in itself a form of nonviolence, whereas imposition would be a subtle form of violent coercion. By showing consideration of their ability to make good decisions we are teaching them to consider and respect others. At the same time, we are helping them to formulate their own good decisions rather than to rely on the experts. But above all, through respect for, consideration of and confidence in them we are displaying our love. As Albert Einstein said, "I would teach peace rather than war. I would inculcate love rather than hate."

8

Spirituality in the Family

> I hate, I despise your feasts,
>   and I take no delight in your
>   solemn assemblies . . .
> Take away from me the noise
>   of your songs;
>   to the melody of your harps
>   I will not listen.
> But let justice roll down like waters,
>   and righteousness like an
>   overflowing stream...
>   —*Amos5:21,23-24.*

It was a balmy California day when we gathered in our backyard for Mark's First Communion Mass. Friends from the Pacific Life Community and the Catholic Worker came to help us celebrate along with Mimi and Pappy, Mark's grandparents. We clustered together as the liturgy began—sitting on the grass or lawn chairs. Next to Father Larry at the tiny improvised altar sat Mark, wearing the "peace cross" we had given him as a remembrance of this day. A red homemade candle molded into a coconut shell was on the altar—Mark's First Communion candle.

Mark read a short Bible passage we had chosen together as appropriate for this occasion and his sister Mary read from Jonathan Livingston Seagull. Appropriately, Father Larry chose the gospel message from St. Mark. Then Mark received communion for the first time under the apricot tree with the birds chirping overhead.

When the last hymn was sung, we followed the liturgical celebration with a feast of tostadas and punch. The Mexican flavor gave this joyous occasion a festive atmosphere, but it was a day Mark will remember for a lifetime.

If Gandhi is correct that nonviolence is a state of active love and St. John equates love to God, it then follows that a connection between nonviolence and spirituality exists. We believe it does and find that fostering spirituality is the surest means of reducing violence. Whether such fostering be in the Christian tradition or some other credible faith seems to make little difference. The basic method of love is the same in all.

Although a healthy sense of spirituality is needed for a balanced personality, not everyone acknowledges this. Too often people look at what can be rationally and logically proven, neglecting the concept of a supreme creator who is responsible for nature and humanity. While many of us flock to church every week in a more or less conditioned response to preached doctrine— accepting ready-made formulae for religious behavior— we seldom become enchanted by the mysteries of a supernatural spirit. Too often our preoccupation with fulfilling ritualistic practices leaves us no time to thirst for insight into the spiritual mysteries. For many religious practice has degenerated to superficial activities such as wearing religious medals, lighting candles and fulfilling Sunday "obligations."

Those who pack the churches on Sunday mornings are a significant number and their effect on society could be substantial. Yet the rising crime rate and the increasing disparity between rich and poor continue virtually unimpeded. The majority of churchgoers neither threaten our exploitive national life-style nor challenge a government which grants tax exemptions provided that religion does not meddle in politics or state affairs. While religions usually do not exempt the state from their teachings, in practice those teachings are not taken seriously.

One friend who was working to stop production of Trident nuclear missiles and submarines highlighted this separation of religion from politics in a letter. Describing attempts to work through churches:

> "We began approaching the churches . . . and without
> fail every single minister agreed there was genuine

cause for concern and perhaps responsible Christians should be involved BUT refused to let us meet with any of the study groups or organizations in their church. One of the ministers I spoke with was a retired Navy chaplain and was in total agreement as far as [the] Trident being [a] first strike [weapon], yet did not want to risk offending any members of his congregation by including what they would view as anti-American activities in the church."

No wonder the widespread belief that institutionalized religion has to a large degree been co-opted by the state so that churchgoers become psychologically anesthetized as they sedulously scurry about fulfilling religious exercises of superficial consequence with no perspective of the overview. People go to church, hear about things that happened centuries ago (with only vague hints about their relevancy today), sing inspirational songs, enjoy congenial companionship and bask in their own good fortune of being among the saved. They leave church feeling comfortable, with little inkling of how their own life-style oppresses the poor whom Jesus called blessed. Such an impervious attitude is far removed from those early Christians in the catacombs who suffered persecution and torturous death for living out the teachings of Jesus.

The opposite of America's non-awareness is manifested in countries where human rights are suppressed and religious leaders will not be compromised. Governments then find religion a potent force with which to deal. Cardinal Jaime L. Sin of Manila said from the heart of the former Marcos dictatorship in the Philippines, "If the human rights of the people are violated by the state, then ipso facto, the church present in the people becomes involved. If the freedom of the people to organize, to express dissent, to be authentically represented is curtailed, then the church stands by their side as advocate. If the state does not abide by the people's mandate to establish on our fair land a regime of justice, peace, liberty and equality—as stated in the Preamble of our Constitution—then the people's demand becomes also the church's demand."

In the face of such firm, spiritual resistance a repressive government, whether communist or fascist, must proceed softly or it will have an insurgency on its hands. The trouble with all governments in existence whether they espouse communism, socialism, capitalism, fascism, is their one-sided view of economics as only pertaining to the means of production and controlling the same. This ambition dominates all other values—including a just distribution of resources motivated by the intent to meet everyone's needs, along with judicious use of resources so that future generations will not be wanting.

Economics not practiced in totality is not true economics, but when it is applied as an aesthetic value, it moves into proper perspective with other social, spiritual, moral and physical values. Just as a person who focuses on materialism and physical beauty is unhealthy, a society looking primarily on how the means of production are controlled is headed for trouble. The right things need to be produced for the right purposes. It is a sickness to specialize in trade, maximize output or economize operations when unemployment is rising and portions of the population are living in poverty.

The true practice of religion addresses all attributes of the individual personality and of the social makeup. It is more than just pious exercises. We have been influenced by many of the world's religions although we profess Christianity—mainly because Christian traditions relate best to our personal background and the Western culture in which we live. But we cannot put God in a box nor demand God's truth be revealed in only one manner or in only one syntax. Disagreements between religions seem to occur over how people interpret that truth and these interpretations too often become stagnated in traditions that warp a dynamic spirituality which calls for continual searching. This stagnated belief then becomes twisted to accommodate the prevailing mores of society. Such faulty interpretations can be seen in the wars which have been fought for religious reasons—both opponents believing that God, as perceived by them, is on their side. Human interpretations, passing as religion, are the true opiate of the people's consciences. Faulty interpretations can mask the real message of love and compassion while leaving unchallenged a society where violence flourishes and power is equated to wealth.

These are the obstacles parents face when trying to bring spirituality and nonviolence into the family community. This is where we must stand firm and make the best judgments possible. If we are to deposit our children into a culture with more than a desire for economic competition, then spirituality must flourish at the foundation level. This spirituality has to be a sincere search for the truth. It can also be challenging and exciting.

When we first married we were very curious about religion. Bob was taking instructions to become a Catholic and Janet tried to explain her faith to him. As children were given to us they were taught to love Jesus and obey his laws. In our experience we found that it was not hard for our children to relate to the "baby Jesus" born in the stable, but we encountered a bigger and more important challenge in helping older youth relate to the radical Jesus in his maturity. It was difficult even for us to relate to the true gospel message.

As our older children reached school age we enrolled them in Catholic school. When we moved to our present home in Santa Clara, we scoured the valley looking for openings in parochial schools, taking very literally our obligation to give our children a Catholic education. Finally we were able to enroll Janie, our oldest daughter, in a Catholic school in downtown San Jose while Cres, our oldest son, was admitted to another Catholic school in a different part of San Jose. Every day these two rode their bikes a mile and a half to the bus stop, took the public bus to the center of San Jose, transferred to another that went to their schools, and walked the final few blocks.

When Jim was ready for first grade, we were able to enroll him in a Catholic school in Santa Clara. Danny was the first one to be accepted in our own parish school. By the time Kathy was in kindergarten we had children in five different schools. Later, these same five would attend five different high schools. Danny and Kathy each started in Catholic high schools and later transferred to public, for reasons we will explain later.

Kathy, Teri and Mary all went to our parish's school although Kathy was the only one of the three who finished all eight grades there. As you can see, we went to tremendous effort and expense to do what we thought was right at that time. Not only did we believe it was necessary for the good of all our souls, but Catholic schools tended to reinforce our values. We looked for the right authority to follow and, also, we were authoritarian parents. But slowly we began to change as consciousness of a better authority grew.

Shortly after we moved to Santa Clara we were invited to join the Christian Family Movement. In this program of observe-judge-act we investigated many aspects of family life before branching out into study of the social, political and economic spheres. By working closely with other couples in CFM we became acutely aware of the family's importance in the world.

As we became more involved in the church, Pope John XXIII, as theologians explained, began to open a window of the church to let in a little fresh air. Mainly he accomplished this by calling the Second Vatican Council which touched off incredible reform in the church so that many things which the CFM had been experimenting with were implemented as church policy. Unfortunately this was also the beginning of a polarization into the Catholic "right" and "left." The resulting debates on what religion is all about helped us to see that many of the Christian traditions we lived with had been implemented as disciplines rather than being instituted by Christ. As such we felt that they were not to be set in concrete, so in a real sense we ourselves became pilgrims searching for the truth.

During this period of the early 1960s we went on a Cursillo retreat. Their goal was to give us a condensed experience of a model Christian community, providing us more insight to the gospel messages. Piety, study and action were the three elements the Cursillo experience tried to bring to our everyday lives. Finding a new awareness of Jesus' love while studying the needs of our brothers and sisters in the human family certainly did lead to new and different types of action for us. It started in the adult education program of our parish but we soon reached the limit of what our pastor would allow. We then experimented with lay communities and participated in lay reform movements. This eventually led to active resistance to the violence in our society and even to the point of arrest for citizen intervention and brief stays in jail.

During our involvement with liturgical communities Diane and Nancy, our youngest daughters, reached the age to receive Holy Communion. Their experience was in contrast to our older children who had dressed in white—with veils for the girls and ties for the boys. After practicing long hours to perform the ceremony with precision, our older ones were so nervous about how to walk, genuflect and turn around that it didn't seem they could really appreciate the sacrament. Thus we decided that with Diane and Nancy we would quietly invite them to receive communion with us and make it a natural event.

We now feel this overreaction to the strict ceremonial format was probably a mistake. Since this is an important religious rite of passage, making it a special celibratory occasion is appropriate. Diane and Nancy still probably regret that they did not have a new dress and veil for the occasion as their older sisters did and certainly were cheated out of the ceremony and celebration. Thus we planned a more festive occasion when Mark's time came.

Changes with the children's education proceeded in much the same manner as our religious observance. One of the first things we did when the fresh air began to blow into our religious world was to reevaluate the Catholic education system. Academically it was superior to public schools so we could find no fault there. Likewise we appreciated these schools for teaching values, although they seemed to oversaturate students with religious doctrine before they had developed a yearning for it. But the cost of a Catholic education made it unavailable to low income families, although scholarships were arranged for a lucky few. The children from active Catholic families (active participation in church functions was a prerequisite for enrollment) were isolated in Catholic schools which meant their influence was not reaching the public education milieu. In short, we were enjoying a privilege because we could afford it while at the same time we were losing contact with the secular society.

After much thought we decided to move Teri and Mary to public schools and Kathy to a public high school. Next came the question of formal religious education. Our church teaches that parents must, under pain of what they label as mortal sin, give their children a religious education. This is generally interpreted as attending a Catholic school or enrolling in religious education (catechism) classes. By this time we could see that the dogmatic approach incorporated into traditional Catholic education had caused a bitterness in our older children because of the "fear of God" that was impressed upon them. At the same time, we could see in our younger kids a craving to learn about the wonders of the universe. Our concern became how to nourish their desire for knowledge without stifling it with a deluge of unsolicited information. We decided to allow our children to proceed at their own pace by giving them information when they were motivated to accept it—which led to keeping them away from catechism classes. It seemed to us that participation in these classes should be their choice. Yet we faced a dilemma. By not allowing them to attend when they were motivated, it seemed they might be missing discussions with their peers and adults other than us. On the other hand, allowing the younger ones to attend voluntarily could result in their receiving so much structured training that it would squelch their thirst for knowledge.

Often as parents we don't have enough faith in our own spiritual beliefs. If we could trust our faith experiences we could believe that God's message would shine through even if it takes many years longer than we would like, and even if our children at first experiment with ideas different than ours. In today's instant society we want instant conversion and instant salvation; so we are tempted to put pressure on our children to conform, and thereby teach the archaic concept of fear rather than the law of love which Jesus introduced.

It is hard for anyone to feel love for a master who threatens eternal hell if we do not behave. People might conform because they do not want to fry their souls but they do not necessarily love the one who threatens that. What we really need is the patience to work with God in helping our children meet divine truth at their own pace. In order for them to know love they must feel love. It is this God of love and mercy whom we want our children to meet.

Once in discussing spirituality with Janie we could not figure out why we were not communicating. When we asked what God meant to her, she told us she couldn't relate to some old man sitting "up there" ready to strike us down with a lightning bolt if we got out of line. This was the concept conveyed to her during formal religious education and by our own dogmatic approach during Janie's formative years. We could see that spirituality has to be absorbed in the context of living and experiencing life, along with some ritual and prayer.

One way we found helpful in accomplishing this is through liturgical year celebrations—seasonal games, if you will. Playing Christkindl during Advent is one. This German custom to prepares us for the coming of Christ on Christmas by seeing and serving him in others. On the first Sunday of Advent all the family members draw each other's names from a bowl to find out who their secret Christkindl (Christ child) is. Each day of Advent you do something nice for your Christkindl without getting caught and each week you write an anonymous note to your Christkindl telling them of special prayers and sacrifices you are doing. On Christmas you write your Christkindl a letter, signing it to reveal who you are. Our children love playing this game and all the while they are doing nice things for someone else, another person is doing nice things for them. That is what nonviolence is all about.

We have also tried to use more specific ways of observing important dates on the church calendar. Several years ago on Good Friday, for instance, we started to spend the hours from noon until three quietly in the mountains rather than in church. Being in the midst of God's creation during this holy time of reflection seems to help our appreciation of the observance.

Recently we have held Good Friday vigils at Lockheed, right across the street from the building where Trident missiles are being manufactured. Everyone attending is invited to bring readings and thoughts to help us understand better the "modern crucifixion" taking place right now where nuclear missiles are the nails piercing the flesh of humanity. The comparison is vivid and awakening.

Another way of bringing spirituality into every moment of living is through prayer. To give prayer a special meaning, as opposed to habitual patterns of words recited at specific times, we encourage our children to talk to God throughout the day—asking for help with school work, getting along with others, or what have you. Prayer, in our family, has come a long way from swatting the children to make them sit still while we recite a family rosary.

For several years now, we have been involved with "Parenting for Peace and Justice"—a national network, fast becoming international, started by our good friends, Jim and Kathy McGinnis. The movement has the dual goals of helping parents raise children to see that everyone in our global family is taken care of and then to take care of our planet and its resources so that future members of the human family can live a wholesome life. In our experience there is a direct relationship between prayer and parenting for peace and justice. Although prayer means many things to many people—formal prayer, action prayer, prayer through dancing and through songs—still the basic ingredient of prayer is very simple: talking with God. It is something which is done best continuously and spontaneously throughout each day. We believe that Jesus is walking with us at all times so it is only polite to talk with him. Listening for his response is also a part of prayer dialogue.

Formal prayers have their place but one must guard against their becoming mechanical. Prayers said spontaneously are less apt to do that and they are a more natural way of communication. We live on a busy street close to a hospital. Ambulances are continually screaming by. It has been a practice in our family for many years to say a prayer for the sick and the dying, or whomever needs help, every time we hear a siren. This is a very meaningful practice for our children.

There are three main aspects of prayer which we try to teach our children: First, it is a means of thanking God for what we have received. Second, it is an opportunity to express our love for God. And, third, it is an opportunity to ask for help in living the kind of life God wants us to live—with the emphasis on what God wants.

In order to express thanks for the things God has done for us, we must be aware of what was done—thus we must be alert to understand how God affects us through other people. This means appreciating God in nature and counting our blessings (not our money—which is probably the least of our blessings). To be cognizant of how God is helping us we need time just to think. These times of contemplation and introspection are important whether they are in the form of meditation or just letting our mind wander while we play a game of solitaire. The main thing is to be in tune with God's presence, observant of the effect of that presence on us.

Prayer is also an important avenue to convey our love to God. Why do we love God? Possibly because God has been good to us. But how do we love such an abstract and mystical being? It seems reasonable that we have to know someone before we can really relate to that person with love.

So how do we know God? We learn about God from reading the Bible and other books, but that is abstract knowledge. To really know God we have to experience God. We have to be able to see and touch and hear God. At least that is what the rational and logical side of our minds tell us, since there is a little bit of the "doubting Thomas" in most of us.

According to the Christian tradition, we were allowed to experience God physically as incarnated in Jesus. But God is also physically with us today, incarnate in the form of our brothers and sisters in the global family. Jesus told us where to serve divinity—in the poor, the sick, those in jail, the underdogs in society—in short, in human suffering. This requires having contact with the suffering people and bringing our children in contact with them.

Many years ago a Sister Bravo ran a center in the slums of San Jose, California to provide recreation and education for poor children. We used to take our children there to work and play with those children. Nowadays there is the Catholic Worker community which feeds street people and provides homes for single mothers as well as delinquent adolescents. Some of our children assisted at Loaves and Fishes Family Kitchen and at the Emergency Housing Center.

Vacations are also a good opportunity to learn about the poor and suffering. Organized trips for high school students to work with the poor in Mexicali and Tijuana are examples. Family vacations to Appalachia and other poverty areas also help us and our children to know God. All of this becomes a form of prayer. By showing our concern for the poor and suffering we are saying that we love God. Ironically, in our experience we have always found we gained much more from these encounters than we gave.

Another way to experience and love God is through the beauty of nature—discovering how the turtle lays its eggs so they will be protected; how the spider spins its web; what makes the grass grow and become green? The opportunities to experience God in nature are limitless. Albert Einstein, often referred to as an atheist, explained his experiencing of God: "My religion consists of a humble admiration of the illimitable superior spirit who reveals Himself in the slight details we are able to perceive with our frail and feeble minds."

Another part of prayer is asking God's guidance and grace to live a life of truth. Too often prayer gets to be an endless petition for things we want: "Please help me to get a raise so we can buy a house like the Jones's." "Please God, get me a new doll like Alice's." "Please Jesus, help me get a personal computer so I can play video games."

What God wants us to do and how God wants us to act is not always easy to recognize. More times than not it is downright hard. But the emphasis here is on what God wants, not what we want. The main thing we should pray for is the grace to accept God's will. Before we can do this, however, we must know what that will is. That is why we ask for help in what to do and how to act. For God to be able to show us these things introduces another aspect of prayer—listening. Again we have to be alert and aware—two essential parts of prayer—if we are to carry on a real conversation with God.

Sometimes we have to listen through quietness, reflection, contemplation, meditation, even daydreaming. But in many instances we receive God's guidance through everyday events—usually a series of mundane occurrences, not cataclysmic miracles. We have to watch for these signposts and try to interpret them. This, of course, means paying attention to what is happening. Our Buddhist brothers and sisters call it "mindfulness."

There are some clues we should watch for. Sometimes things just do not work out no matter how hard we try. Rather than continuing to fight against it, maybe we should ask what God is trying to tell us through these impediments. Our response then should be to reevaluate our effort and pray for further guidance.

Another marker to look for is the feeling of being uncomfortable. This is a sign that God seems to use frequently to tell us that change is needed. We should then stop and ask why we are uncomfortable. Just as the rich man who felt anxious enough to tell Jesus that although he had obeyed all the religious laws, he wanted to know what else he should do to guarantee perfection. Jesus' response suggested selling all he had, giving the money to the poor, and then coming and following him. The rich man, uncomfortable with that suggestion, went away.

How do we react to the feeling of being uncomfortable?

Another way God speaks to us is through a pattern of "coincidences" occurring. These incidents are usually so trivial that it would be embarrassing to convince another person that they have meaning. Yet if we pay attention to them we sometimes find a message.

Just remembering to pray for enlightenment is probably the most important part of all. Many times we have struggled to make a decision or solve a problem on our own, to no avail. But when we remember to ask God to help, the solution often jumps right out. When it comes to responding, we just have to trust God enough to accept the message on faith, even though we might not be able to see the outcome at that time.

There is no secret formula for prayer. Actually, what we have presented here is not new. But these are means which have worked for us and our family. Awareness and participation in the struggle for peace and justice requires action in the world and action is an important ingredient of prayer. Action is our response to God's guidance which we so prayerfully seek and is, in itself, a further extension of prayer—showing our love to God by responding to God's desires as we understand them.

To stimulate spiritual experiences in our family, in the atmosphere of modern living and during the time of forming values, has been an important goal for us. In all this we have tried to maintain that balance of guidance and choice so the whole process avoids becoming coercive. When that balance is obtained, the children can see the value of ritual and tradition as well as their function in the world in which they live.

By the time Mark was eight years old he barely knew the Lord's Prayer. Maybe we were neglectful in that but he was really curious and interested about prayer. He wrote this poem:

> A child that lives,
> A child that dies,
> Is never dead,
> because his spirit
>   still lives.
>   —By Mark, 8 years old.

Such responses from our children are rewarding for they indicate that somehow we are providing the atmosphere for getting the idea across of what prayer is all about.

9

Large Families

I am a part of the sun
         as my eye is part of me.
That I am part of the earth
         my feet know perfectly,
And my blood is part of the sea.
My soul knows that I am
         part of the human race,
My soul is an organic part
         of the great human race.
As my spirit is part of my nation.
In my own very self
         I am part of my family.
         —*David Herbert Lawrence*
         Apocalypse

Diane and Nancy slipped under the altar and waved at the congregation while our attention was on Mark's baptismal ceremony. Two women later fluently expressed their disapproval of such "disrespect." The baptismal party then moved to Mark's godparents' house for refreshments. Their eleven children combined with our ten created a high decibel affair. The uninitiated would likely throw up their hands in despair.

Incidents like these have generated a stereotype of chaos associated with large families. Frequent spats are readily recognized as manifestations of violence when numerous children are concentrated under one roof. Smaller families are seemingly more peaceful.

To some extent this is true but there seems to be more to the story. Our experience indicates that such disorder can be creative in the long run. Earlier we explained how children need to work frustrations out in fantasy so they don't gain monumental proportions later in life. A similar analogy applies to coping with violent tendencies. Interaction with siblings during the early years prepares children for constructive participation in society later on. Little by little, after many tiffs and clashes—severity of which depends on the quality of parental guidance—a reckoning seems to be reached and understanding of each other's feelings takes place. Large families offer an opportunity for wider loving interaction and, as we have observed, this stimulates more compassion later in the broader community.

We love each of our ten children beyond description. Many times we have been teased about our Catholic beliefs being the reason for our large family. Even though this had something to do with it, an equally plausible reason was our love for each other and our desire to have children. We used to say that we wanted a dozen, but we fell a couple short of that aspiration. We did stop for a little while after Mary, our seventh child, was born, but by the time she was five we decided we wanted more. Diane was born as Mary started kindergarten and that filled what would have been a void in the house during the day. Nancy and Mark joined us at the end of the 60s.

This chapter is not meant to be a pep talk in favor of large families. Each couple must decide for themselves how many children they want to raise and whether they want natural or adopted children. But in the hope that we can help others make a better informed decision we would like to share some of our pilgrimage. There are many good things along with some sticky points to ponder for those who aspire to have a large family. World population problems, which are well known, of course need to be considered. Had there been more consciousness of population growth in our younger days, it possibly would have affected our plans. Possibly! On the other hand we are not convinced that the Malthusian philosophy is as applicable to humanity as some would have us believe. In a world having less greed and less wasteful consumption of resources, and with a value structure oriented toward people rather than possessions, this planet could support many more people than it does at present. Too often, it seems to us, the limiting of population is motivated by the hope of sustaining an affluent life-style without depletion of resources.

Aside from these issues, the most obvious difficulty with a large family is finding the physical stamina to spread enormous amounts of care and attention to numerous children. Not only do we feel that it is important for parents to provide time alone with each child, it is also good to allow each one time alone with their grandparents, aunts and uncles. Danny used to really appreciate visiting his grandparents by himself, and once remarked to them, "It sure is good to be lonely." He enjoyed the stability of a second home of love, as did all the children.

Providing individual attention can be a problem at times—especially in those chaotic moments when all are crying for attention at once. Having several sick simultaneously (a not uncommon experience in a large family) is a real drain on the patience and strength of a parent. When it comes to parental participation at the children's social and community activities—open house at the schools and performances in special events—Murphy's law usually arranges two or three programs to occur at the same time. Quite often we would split up to cover as many as possible, dashing from one to another, leaving some early and arriving late at others. Strenuous as this might be, it is vital to developing children that their parents be interested in their activities. When this energy is expended with the right attitude it can turn into a loving experience of service and teaching nonviolence.

All is not difficult, however. Some things work in favor of a large family today, such as a moderate amount of technology. Modern washing machines, stoves and permanent press clothing, to name a few, drastically cut down on the physical chores associated with child raising. It is when technology is perpetuated for its own sake, or for the sake of excessive profits at the expense of other people, that it becomes evil.

A real plus for large families, at least in our experience, is more on the metaphysical level and is called love—in our vocabulary another term for nonviolence. Love energy must be viewed differently from physical energy. Whereas the latter can be depleted by the demands of many children, that is not the case with love. We have never had a problem with loving each of our ten children just as much as if they had been an only child. The wonderful and mysterious thing about love is that the more you give away, the more you get. It is truly a nondepletable spiritual resource.

Difficulties sometimes arise with the showing of love, which gets back to the physical energies of the parent. Showing love is closely linked with the feeling and existence of love—which is always a fragile and delicate commodity. Love has to be nourished and tended with extreme care. In order for it to flourish it must be shared and exhibited, and that takes a physical and mental effort. Children, just like all people, need to be told time and time again that they are loved. Making sure that the words do not grow stale requires ingenuity. Often we demonstrate our love with deeds, acts of kindness, caring—in short, the demonstration of love takes a conscious and physical effort. When our fear of being overwhelmed with activity and fatigue is surmounted by sheer will and effort, we are immediately flooded with more of that indescribable feeling of greater love.

We once heard this phenomenon compared to a bucket full of rocks filled with water. As we throw out the rocks there is more room for water. The rocks represent our worldly cares and limitations and the water is love. As we empty ourselves of our self-interests we can hold more love. This is the essence of the Biblical saying that we must empty ourselves in order to be filled. As we are filled, our love shines in a purer sense on our children. To accomplish this expunging of worldly interests, however, parents need time for recreation—time to re-create their energies. Sleep and rest are essential to restoring our physical energy. Likewise parents need time alone—sometimes together and sometimes separated—to restore their emotional energy. We have always been better at arranging times to be away together than times of absolute solitude.

Admittedly, there are difficulties experienced by and in large families. Housing is one. It is very expensive and, like food, is being manipulated to reap massive profits. The odds are against children in a large family enjoying the privacy of separate rooms. Some people do not look upon this as a problem because they feel private rooms are a luxury and sharing creates a sense of community. That philosophy may have some valid points but we are more inclined to believe that each human being is entitled to some small space which they can call their own—some place always available for meditation, thinking or just getting away from others for a while.

Adequate housing does not mean a mansion. Both of us were raised in humble homes and believe it is the love that fills the home, not the structure itself, that matters. Overcoming inconveniences and hardships, done with the right attitude, can be transformed into sharing and mutual accomplishments. More so to children than anyone, feeling love is the most important catalyst for such accomplishments.

Another difficult aspect of a large family is the length of time it takes to raise many children. Parents with only two or three children find their child rearing days drawing to a close while in their early 40s. We will be in or close to our 60s before our youngest child reaches the age of majority. This call on our physical energies over an extended period and into our advancing age makes it harder to keep up with all the activities demanded of a parent. In many ways our younger children have been deprived of some parental companionship by having older parents. Nevertheless, they seem to love and appreciate us just as much even though we are old fogy parents.

Blessings accompany every difficulty. Younger children in a large family have older brothers and sisters who, we have found, are more than anxious to do things with the smaller ones. They take their little brother and sisters fishing, hiking and backpacking—to play ball, jog and go shopping. Our younger children have always looked forward to an overnight, and sometimes longer, visit with an older brother or sister—or brother-in-law or sister-in-law. Even baby-sitting with the nieces and nephews is a big thing. As much as our younger children love us, they are always eager to get away with our older ones. This community atmosphere in our family is a beautiful relationship and has provided many fulfilling moments for us.

A slightly different situation exists when very young children are living in the same house with teenagers. Gearing a household to toddlers and primary graders while at the same time providing a wholesome atmosphere of experimentation for adolescents provides some difficulties. Although not a serious problem, awareness of the situation is required as is more intense parenting. The difference in freedom allowed is one source of disharmony. Little ones find it difficult to understand the age difference and the accompanying responsibility when teenagers are allowed a greater selection of television viewing or are given more freedom in choosing places they wish to go. From another viewpoint, when those in their teen years are struggling against limits, their release of emotions is often a poor example for younger siblings. It is a constant challenge to properly channel that release of adolescent energy.

Again there is a sunny side. Children do learn to adapt to different age groups and varying situations. Having a wide age spread at home is an excellent opportunity for teenagers to show and receive affection without being embarrassed. They like to be hugged and little ones love to hug. Many youth never have a chance to care for small children and the opportunity to do so is a wholesome learning experience. They soon find out how dependent tiny tots are and, with good guidance, can learn nonviolent forms of discipline which will be helpful in later years with their own families.

Large families do bring much joy and fulfillment to parents despite the long and often tedious struggle to raise the children. It really does seem to us that people from large families know better how to get along with others in community and in society. Our children do have a caring concern for others and that is a good thing to see.

There are also those rewarding times when appreciation for our care over the years is outwardly shown—although parents do not raise children for reward. One Christmas Janet received a "Mother's Ring" with ten birthstones—one for each of the children's birthdays. Having conspired in planning this unique gift the children discovered that rings with ten birthstones are not exactly common, so it did not arrive in time for Christmas. However, to have something for her on Christmas day, each of the children wrote a note telling how much their mother meant to them. These individual expressions of love were given to Janet, who still says it was one of the most meaningful gifts she ever received.

There are always the little day-to-day things which children are so good at doing to show love—multiplied tenfold in our case. Notes have been a prominent medium of expression in our family. Many times a surprise note will appear in our lunch bag. Nancy once hid a note in Bob's suitcase, dotting all the "i"s with miniature hearts:

> Dear Dad,
>
> How are you doing. I am doing fine. I am writing a story for Miss Wilkenson, my teacher. We all miss you. We love you too. We are fine in school. Mark has a letter for you too as you can see. Mimi reads us the story called "The Story of Jesus."
>
> From Nancy
> XXXXXXXXXX
> OOOOOOOOOO
> P.S. We will be glad when you come back.

Most of all, we wish to emphasize that none of the difficulties encountered in raising a large family are insurmountable. We chose to face those difficulties and are happy to have experienced them. For every inconvenience we encountered there always was at least one compensating asset. With a little awareness and ingenuity, practically every situation can be turned into a healthy event so it is not difficult to make the assets outweigh the problems.

10

Family Actions

The family only represents one aspect, however important an aspect, of a human being's functions and activities. . . . A life is beautiful and ideal, or the reverse, only when we have taken into our consideration the social as well as the family relationship.
—*Havelock Ellis*
Little Essays of Love and Virtue (1922)

Shortly after we ceased to earn our livelihood from the war industry, a friend referred to our family as "refugees in the flight from immorality." Those words described well our feelings at the time and they portend the plight of those who listen to their conscience in today's increasingly militaristic world. Swimming against the tide of public opinion is no easy task. Doing it as a family can result in mutual support if it is done with care. When unity is fostered by mutual love, respect and communication, the binding energy is powerful in the struggle for peace and justice. It is impossible for us to outline a plan of action to fit every family's circumstances, however. There is no universal formula because the degree and rate at which various families, and individuals within the family, can change is not the same. The important thing is that change be uniform within the family so that no member is left behind to feel alienated or different. This does not mean that each member should be the same or feel the same but, rather, that all members should understand and empathize with each other.

Nonviolence has in addition to interior personality traits the outward dimension of public witness. As children develop nonviolent characters it follows naturally that this quality will seek an outlet. This can best be guided through family actions—first within the family and then as a family into the wider community. We feel that extending into society is absolutely necessary if our children are to eventually become responsible citizens.

Over the past years our family has experimented with various actions in our attempt to bring ourselves more in line with a nonviolent and nonexploitive life-style. At this point the pressure of peer groups on youngsters is a critical consideration. Family meetings and good communication are vital in preserving family unity during change. There must also be a constant awareness that the various family members usually progress at different rates. Much of our family's efforts pertain to consuming less. Cutting down on waste is important to peace and justice, and so are environmental concerns. These are probably the most basic of all actions because they start by eliminating selfishness right at our individual cores.

One children's story which has been a favorite of ours is about a boy named Herman who wanted a picture on the wall of his room. Wanting the biggest picture possible, he set about obtaining brushes and paint so he could start drawing trees and houses with a road running through them. He became so enthralled in his fantasy that he stepped up into the picture so he could reach higher to paint the moon. While standing knee deep in buildings he looked down and cried: "I'm a giant!"

Not wanting to frighten the sleeping townspeople, he painted his way out into the hills and around the corner into valleys where he created an ocean and waded right through. Nothing stopped him. On the far side he sketched tall mountains but he was even taller. As he continued, Herman made a pass through these mountains which was just right for a railroad. He painted some tracks—small at first in the distance and then larger and larger as they came closer down the valley. He also painted flowers and grass and birds along the way. Soon the tracks were so big that he was not a giant anymore. He was small—very small—smaller even than the flowers and the birds and . . . (gulp) one of those birds was watching him with a menacing eye. Herman was afraid. He wanted to go back and start over but he was now too small to step over mountains and wade through oceans.

He felt trapped in his own creation. At that moment he came to his senses. Herman picked up his brush and, with two broad strokes, crossed out that picture.

This silly little fable reminds us of how easily reality can become distorted to make us prisoners of our own activity and illustrates how we can be consumed by our created circumstances. It was a liberating experience to recognize the conditions this story brought to mind—the forces which moved us from dependence on weapons building. But even shaking off the shackles of the war industry did not free us from other entanglements. Sometimes it takes more than a couple of strokes to cross out the picture we have painted of our lives.

As in the gospel story of the rich man who asked Jesus how to serve God better, we feel ourselves like the man who could not sell all and follow Jesus, as Jesus advised, because he had many possessions. We often wonder how we would have reacted in that man's place. Parting with our possessions is not easy.

More to the point, how are we responding right now? Jesus' call today is not so direct but it is revealed one step at a time. If we respond we do not find it beyond our ability to follow along. But sometimes we lag behind and become overwhelmed. Or maybe we plan our own steps too rigidly. Call it what you will—resistance to change, lack of faith, love of the good life—but when we falter it is all the harder to catch up. Soon we are so many paces behind that the obstacles to overcome in catching up take on overwhelming proportions. Yet catch up we must if we are to embody our faith. We have the freedom to paint our own picture and take one step at a time. The important thing is to keep stepping.

When Bob abandoned his career of designing missiles we thought this would be the apex of our moral struggle. We were wrong. Healthy spirituality doesn't rest long on one plateau, and neither do the children's appetites. We started cutting expenses while we learned new jobs which would be more helpful to humanity. At first we viewed this belt-tightening as a temporary condition until we could reestablish ourselves on the economic ladder. We found ways to reduce spending and we explored new approaches to pleasure without having to buy entertainment. We also experimented with different diets using less expensive and more ecology-oriented recipes. Soon a pattern took shape and we became aware that simple living in itself is the most direct approach to solving world injustices.

With us, the process of reducing our needs began by revising our work patterns. In its traditional sense, work occupies almost half of our waking hours. We tend to center our lives around the job and fail to see our labor in proper context. We give wage earning undue priority without recognizing that family and friends also deserve prime time. Meaningful recreation and social actions are relegated to spare time activity. Henry David Thoreau succinctly described the plight of affluent America:

> The rich [person] . . . is always sold to the institution which makes him rich. Absolutely speaking, the more money, the less virtue; for money comes between man and his objects, and obtains them for him . . . It puts to rest many questions which he would otherwise be taxed to answer; while the only new question which it puts is the hard and superfluous one, how to spend it. Thus his moral ground is taken from under his feet. The opportunities of living are diminished in proportion to what are called the "means" are increased.

Work has become an end in itself rather than a means of living. We had been so steeped in the necessity for a career and financial security that occupational success had become the paramount goal. This had an anesthetizing effect on our moral perspectives, while job demands tended to preclude opportunities for other functions, including meaningful recreation.

Recreation (re-creation) of our total person is more than pleasure—work is often quite pleasing. Neither does recreation necessarily imply entertainment. Entertainment has a passive connotation whereas recreation needs to be dynamic. Recreation is a change of pace—such as encounters with nature, relaxing interactions with others who hold common beliefs and values or doing something that we find refreshing.

In a more analytical sense, we could say that recreation addresses or exercises those aspects of our personality which we have been neglecting. At work we put a drain on intellectual and/or physical labor. To restore balance, these attributes should be rested while exercising our social tendencies, releasing emotions and gaining spiritual and moral fulfillment. Of course our entire personality should ideally be integrated into our work, but that is not always possible to the fullest degree. As we strive for change we should attempt to incorporate all of these various personality components in all our activity.

Then all too often the success of our work is measured by income. Yet living on a large salary does violence to the 95 percent of the world's population who must survive on only half the global wealth. We sometimes attempt to alleviate our concern about this disparity by donations to "charity," but that type of giving merely numbs our conscience and in no way approaches "charity" (love) in its religious sense. Ambrose, bishop of Milan during the fourth century, said about this token giving, "You are not making a gift of your possessions to the poor. You are handing over to them what is theirs. For what has been given in common for the use of all, you have arrogated to yourself."

That charge puts a different perspective on riches. Most people can readily concede that acquiring wealth by certain methods can be immoral, but usually they will recognize "ethical" means of amassing a fortune. Ambrose debunked this myth. Merely possessing a lot of money (or food or belongings) means having more than one's share, making someone else do without. In short, having more than our immediate needs is possessing something which belongs to someone else. That is why Jesus told the rich man to sell all and give the money to the poor.

There are theoretical arguments that one can live simply on a large salary while using the excess for good works. But voluntary poverty is not comfortable for the affluent and our judgment of what we need is easily distorted. Too often worldly excesses are rationalized away by the "poverty in spirit" alibi. But a spirit of poverty amid wealth is a contradiction. Voluntary poverty does not mean destitution, but it does mean putting our whole being into the act.

Another dream is that we can raise everyone to the American standard of living. This simply is not realistic. This planet is a closed ecosystem and we are straining it right now by depleting resources faster than they can be renewed. Thousands die from malnutrition daily. Hunger accounts for one out of every three deaths in the world today. The 1980s were forecast as the decade of famine, yet there would really be no shortage of food in the world if production and distribution were managed for the benefit of everyone. We need only look at the abundance in the local supermarket to realize that the food industry is big business. Consequently, food accumulates in the areas of the world where there is money to buy it.

In addition to the food problem, it is necessary to consider increasing pollution and the energy shortage which would occur if everyone started burning up resources at the American pace. Depletion would be 20 times the present US consumption. Key resources would be gone in a few decades and the human race would face extinction from the resulting imbalance of nature. At America's standard this planet could only support a half-billion people. With the present global population expected to top ten billion by early in the 21st century, raising the world to the US level of comfort cannot be the answer. Justice dictates that we in developed countries support a just distribution of resources by living more simply.

Simplicity has its advantages. In addition to providing a more equitable distribution, voluntarily consuming only what we need would remove greed from our national makeup—a greed which grows with acquired wealth. Moreover, by living simply we do not have to spend so much time working to support an exploitive life-style. This gives us more time to do some of the things we like to do and to work for peace and justice in the world.

One of the greatest advantages to simple living, however, is that it has freed us to make moral decisions objectively. We are, in Thoreau's terms, not sold to any institution. A common dilemma today is that our government makes demands of us that put us in competition with our brothers and sisters in other lands. One such exaction is the federal income tax, over half of which is used for military purposes. But with our small income we try to stay low in the taxable level so we are not giving financial support to death, destruction and exploitation.

Another portion of our tax dollar is used for foreign aid which has now been manipulated to guarantee a market for US goods. Shortly after the Indochina war, for instance, the US Government bought $25-million worth of tobacco and shipped it to poor countries under the "Food For Peace" program. In this fashion, money intended to feed the hungry was used to insure profits for American tobacco growers at a time when cigarette sales were declining. Eugene R. Black, former president and chair of the World Bank, underscored how US foreign aid is used to benefit American industry:

1) Foreign aid provides a substantial and immediate market for US goods and services.

2) Foreign aid stimulates the development of new overseas markets for US companies.

3) Foreign aid orients national economics toward a free enterprise system in which US firms can prosper.

It is unfortunate that our tax money is buying sophisticated merchandise and irrelevant goods for poor countries when they really need cheap, easily maintained equipment for development and basic foods for survival. Meanwhile, America basks in luxury. When we raise children to fit into this pattern we are teaching them violence against the poor.

A close examination of the high level of buying by Americans reveals that fear of losing the ability to consume actually escalates consumption. To allay that fear, people buy protection (watchdogs which eat more food, security guards, alarm systems) as well as insurance policies (burglary, liability, disability) as they succumb to the paranoia so prevalent today. We have found that anxiety diminishes when we live in moderation. Insurance policies, bank accounts and savings bonds become less compelling because we have less to lose. Simplicity banishes those fears which breed violence in us as it lessens the disparities which cause others to threaten us. At the same time, withholding investment from banks and insurance companies allows us to identify more closely with people who cannot afford such luxuries. And, perhaps most important of all, by not making those investments we do not support the very institutions which finance the exploitative behavior of large American corporations in undeveloped countries.

One such exploitative adventure is cash cropping in Third World countries where labor and land are cheap. The best soil is acquired for growing them while the indigenous population lacks sufficient acreage to grow its own basic food. Cash cropping works in plantation fashion where the field workers are paid only a few dollars for a twelve-hour day.

Coffee and sugar top the cash crop list, followed by coconuts, pineapple and bananas along with many spices and nuts. Our family, in experimenting with ways to reduce consumption of those items, decided that boycotting cash crops was a first step toward ending the feudal systems which enlarge the gap between rich and poor. This also contributes toward ending the exploitation of land, labor and other resources in poorer countries by US businesses—an exploitation which operates under the protective umbrella of America's formidable military machine.

We found we could do without many cash crops and not feel undue hardship. Coffee is a problem because we like coffee. For awhile we used a bran substitute, but it was not the same. Finally we decided to compromise with moderation, rather than dispense with the coffee bean altogether. Sometimes it is possible to buy coffee from countries which are struggling for self-determination, such as Nicaragua. In such cases we help the Third World by buying their product.

Closely related to cash crops is protein waste here at home. Grazing animals can convert grass, and other things humans don't eat, into meat protein. But, to accelerate meat production, cattle raisers have altered the natural food chain. Cattle now have to spend their lifetimes in crowded feed lots where they are force-fed to fatten them up quickly. In our country we feed 78 percent of our basic food grains to livestock. To produce one pound of beef protein requires 21 pounds of plant protein. With more efficient and more humanitarian distribution of those grains, we could go a long way toward reducing hunger in the Third World. To use the primary source of protein more efficiently, and to boycott an industry that treats animals cruelly, our family is experimenting with meatless recipes which are also less expensive. Savoring those well prepared dishes greatly reduces our craving for animal flesh. We frequently serve beans and rice together because legumes and grains complement each other to make more of the available protein useable for our bodies. Taste is also complemented. The whole area of diet is exciting and challenging and fun.

Upon first consideration, it would seem that eggs are a good source of protein which are not exploitative. If you know where the eggs come from that could be true. Most large egg producers, unfortunately, use the cruel practice of forced laying. Several chickens are kept constantly in small cubbyholes with the lights on 24 hours a day. They do not know whether it is day or night and, with constant feeding, often lay a couple of eggs each day. With not even enough room to flap their wings these chickens often beat themselves raw. Breakfast eggs, in our opinion, do not justify such animal cruelty.

There is more than one way to be involved in tax resistance. Keeping our income low to avoid supporting the Pentagon frees us from supporting war making. This is not always easy to do, for it is surprising how many ways to earn money are encountered when one tries to reduce income.

Telephone tax resistance is a symbolic action which does not involve much risk. Simply, one refuses to pay the federal excise tax on the phone bill by attaching a short note to your local telephone bill explaining that you are not paying the tax because it was traditionally levied to support the US war making effort. The same procedure is used on the long distance bill. Supposedly the company merely passes the note on to the Internal Revenue Service and removes the tax from your bill. In practice, the tax often appears in the delinquent column of the next bill. You then have to include in your note the reason for not paying the "past due" portion, in addition to explaining why you are not paying the current tax.

We started refusing to pay the telephone tax in 1972, shortly before Bob resigned his job at Lockheed. When we filed our federal income tax return for that year, we had a refund coming because too much was withheld. When we filed our return we enclosed a letter protesting how our taxes were being used. This tipped off the IRS because, before sending our refund check, we received a letter stating that we would be investigated for other taxes which might be due. There must have been either a lot of confusion or a conscientious IRS worker because, on the next day (April Fool's day), we received a check for the full refund.

The following year we had all of our withholding tax coming back and we received the same notice. This time they did collect a little of the telephone tax but not all. However, when we finally received the remainder of our refund, the amount of penalty and interest the government paid us made the check bigger than it would have been in the first place.

Later, the IRS attached Janet's wages for the telephone tax we still owed. At first they could not take anything out because she was not making enough. After receiving a raise, however, the IRS finally collected, little by little, in 1979. Now we have the satisfaction of knowing that our tax provided employment for a collector rather than weapons.

Our American heritage is rich with tax resistance and other types of non-cooperation to correct injustices. In colonial times we had the Boston Tea Party and resistance to the Stamp Act. In the 1800s there was resistance to slavery. More recently, although not as noble, was noncooperation leading to repeal of prohibition and downgrading some marijuana crimes to misdemeanors. Nevertheless, these were cases where the people invoked their will to abolish unpopular government policies. No government can enforce any law without the loyalty and support of the masses. Using nonviolent resistance in such cases is doubly powerful as governments depend on violence as the last resort in law enforcement and do not know how to cope with nonviolence. The more government tries to cope with nonviolence in enforcing an unpopular law, the more it shows its true violent nature, causing the public to sympathize with the nonviolent practitioners. Public support, of course, is necessary for resistance to gain momentum.

There are some activities in which parents and children can participate together. Nonviolent demonstrations are an arena in which unity and convictions can be expressed by the family. Several of our children usually accompany us to vigils and rallies to protest nuclear weapons. As far back as when we first started becoming involved in peace and justice issues we have included the children.

Mark, too young to remember when we pushed him in a stroller down Geary Street in San Francisco during an Indochina war protest march, does remember Good Friday 1978. So do Diane and Nancy. During Lent that year a group of us had been greeting Lockheed employees at the entrances and gateways of their work area. Candles held during those dark, early morning vigils produced a solemn atmosphere. Signs and leaflets conveyed our message. The noon action on Good Friday was the culmination of a six-week Lenten campaign.

On Good Friday morning we trained for the action in our backyard with role playing and rehearsal. Some of the older children played the part of the Lockheed security officers and the police. Six of us went through the motions of pouring our own blood over a black cross atop a cutout of the Trident submarine—the modern Golgotha. When we felt assured that we could perform the action smoothly and nonviolently we moved out to Lockheed.

At noon some 28 of us walked in solemn procession to the front of Lockheed/Navy building #181 which is the headquarters for managing the Trident missile program and in which Trident missile parts were being manufactured. Children and adults alike carried posters. At the doorway we formed two lines—one with posters depicting life, the other with posters illustrating death. Employees walking in and out were asked to choose. After standing vigil a few minutes, we poured our blood and decorated the steps with Easter lilies.

Lockheed security informed us that we were trespassing and asked us to leave. This was the cue for those not willing to be arrested to move outside the fence. Because of the children, we have never entered an arrest situation together—something we would like to share. However, this was Bob's turn so the children and Janet moved to the other side of the property line. Mark was a little apprehensive when he saw his dad arrested.

Later at the police station, those arrested were booked and released on citation. Bob was the last one out and Mark was getting worried. When Father Larry came Mark asked him where his dad was. Father Larry replied, "Oh, he's in there enjoying the party." Mark looked doubtful so Father Larry said, pointing to a policeman coming out, "Ask him." The police officer stopped and Mark asked if his dad was really enjoying a party in there. "Sure thing," said the officer, "they are having a good time but he'll be out pretty soon."

This illustrates the type of rapport established between the police and demonstrators. The party story was not exactly a hoax because our booking "ceremony" is usually done with quite a bit of joking and kidding. But then, the purpose of a nonviolent action is not to overcome anyone but to embark on a search for the truth (and to symbolize this search) in such a manner that all people involved can come together in some form of understanding. Most of our actions have met with some success in this regard.

Such citizen intervention and jail experiences are not totally inconsistent with the responsibilities of parenthood and we feel gratified at how we put the two worlds together. Citizen intervention is referred to by some as civil disobedience. However, when justified by the principle of necessity to avoid a great harm or in compliance with a higher law, such behavior is not disobedient. The jail is certainly a different world from the family environment, but it is not a new experience for Christians attempting to live by the radical word of the gospel. In this vein we explained our actions to the children when they were smaller. They used to follow us through every step leading up to, during and following the nonviolent citizen intervention action. They have seen and frequently have participated in the extensive planning, preparation, prayer and fasting preparatory to such an event. Thus they understand the symbolism of the action and why it is sometimes necessary to break minor laws nonviolently to prevent a greater harm or a more serious crime. Usually after such a citizen intervention event, our children would follow through with us in the preparation for and participation in the trial, which brought home the seriousness of the affair along with our feelings that such actions are the best way we know to carry out our religious convictions. There is little doubt in our children's minds that we are striving to follow Jesus. Given the condition of this country and the world today, risking freedom and possessions is the most potent example parents can set for their children. We also believe that all parents who are really concerned about their children's future may eventually be forced to this extreme. However, if more people would become more conscientiously active in democracy, such extreme intervention measures would probably not be necessary.

Of all the actions mentioned, simple living is the most important as a base from which other activity will follow. We cannot be effective in changing society until we at least initiate change in ourselves and our family. Neither can change happen overnight. It is a step-by-step process. If we pick one thing at a time (such as boycotting a cash crop) and stick with that, additional steps will be revealed. This is better than a big burst of activity which burns out fast. A little spot can smolder for a long time, gradually growing hotter and spreading in the process. When that smoldering spot is ready to burst into a small flame, we will be the ones doing the fanning. The flame will continue to spread into more intensive and effective activity if we are alert to the motivation and respond to it. We should not be overwhelmed by trying to foresee the outcome five or six steps from now. If we just focus on the next step we will have the courage and faith to face each step as it comes.

We found that in order to make a nonviolent event a family affair, it is necessary to allow the children to be part of the action. When we do not buy bananas or pineapple or coconuts, they know why and they realize that our family's money is not being used to exploit others. We help them to feel proud that their clothes are not fancy and that by making them last they are preserving diminishing resources. We stimulate our children to relate to poor people in a personal way. We encourage hope by letting our children know that most people in our society are basically good—just misinformed due to the heavy pressure of political and commercial propaganda. Finally, we try to help the children to recognize that propaganda for what it is so they can make good decisions.

Our family has only scratched the surface in becoming more life affirming, and we have not exhausted all the opportunities for action open to parents and families. We are still feeling our way but we recognize that reducing America's living standard is necessary to achieve justice— and that justice is needed for true peace. We are trying to be less greedy as we search for new ways to cut our needs. We are trying to raise our voice in defense of those who cannot be heard—both the poor in faraway lands and our future generations.

In short, we are very much like Herman when he crossed out his complex fantasy. He then painted a simple picture and was much happier with it. So are we.

11

Fear in the Family

If you won't listen to the adults,
 please
in behalf of the children of the world,
 I beg of you,
give yourselves and us a chance.
— *Gerald Orjuela*
 Age 12, to the US Congress

Fear is a terrible thing. It can be destructive and motivate unnatural behavior. It can inflate circumstances beyond proportion and skew perceptions to where events can seem overwhelming. When this fear happens in young children, it can be devastating. When the family—the sanctuary of comfort and security—is invaded by fear, it affects children in their most vulnerable environment and all sorts of bad things result.

Many surveys have been conducted to determine what fears predominate in children's minds. Although the results of these studies seem to differ in degree, they agree pretty well on the main causes of fear. Two seem to predominate. One is fear that they will lose one or both parents through death or divorce, and the other is fear of nuclear war. To live in the shadow of both creates a destructive force which is often not recognized by child or parents. We are convinced that parents would be shocked if they knew what went through the minds of their children.

The first fear, divorce, is realized in about half the families in our society. According to the National Center for Health Statistics, there were 1.18 million divorces in the United States during 1982. That represents 47 percent of the marriages performed in 1982 and is almost a three-fold increase over 20 years ago. The only hopeful thing about this grim statistic is that, after decades of increasing ratios of divorce to marriage, there is now a small decline. The divorce rate seems to have peaked in 1981 at 51 percent of the marriages performed. Let us hope that this is a continuing trend and that the decreasing ratio will decrease faster.

But this small glimmer of hope is of no avail to the child already caught in the divorce trauma. Even for children whose parents are still together, there is the anxiety of an impending crisis. Given their many friends who have separated parents, divorce appears probable and the slightest squabble between parents creates extreme tension in the child.

This spiral appears self-perpetuating because of the bitterness and cynicism which result from bad marriage experiences. Also, the main cause of divorce can be traced to violence of either a physical or more subtle nature. Violence seems to be the visible manifestation of many complex psychological problems. Physical violence in the family has been well documented by various investigative bodies and some estimate that 50 to 60 percent of today's marriages contain some physical violence. That figure has a startling similarity to divorce statistics.

As we stated earlier, we believe corporal punishment is a form of physical violence. In some families this is carried to the extreme of child abuse. Up to two million children are abused by their parents each year—beaten with fists, kicked, bitten and the like. As many as 700 of those die each year from such treatment. Similar statistics exist for wife-beating. A California report estimates that approximately half of all adult women will be battered at some time in their lives. An estimated 24 million women have been severely beaten at least once by men they live with in intimate relationships. The report warned that if this domestic violence is not detected and remedied, it tends to escalate in both frequency and severity and sometimes leads to homicide.

Children exposed to this experience tend to carry it into their own relationships. The fear of violence in schools is now believed to be disproportionately greater than the number of reported incidents. This has a debilitating effect on the school and those associated with it which is as great as the actual experience of violence itself. It adversely affects teachers and administrators in their functioning and causes students to dislike school, their teachers and other students. It also makes students feel powerless and this leads to social withdrawal, poor academic performance and sometimes delinquent behavior.

This can be the root cause of apathy in later life when citizens should be actively participating to make democracy work. The ultimate conclusion to this situation was experienced at an Alabama high school where a teenager shot a classmate and then killed himself. Fear mounted to the level where metal detectors were used to search for weapons as the students arrived at school.

Let us step back and see what this symptomizes in our culture. Fear leads to body and baggage searches at airports, government buildings and similar places. What kind of society have we when high school students must pass through security checks in order to pursue their education? What sort of learning environment does this provide? How soon will these measures be taken in intermediate and primary grades? Are these fearful reactions addressing the cause of violence?

Unfortunately, we are not facing up to the causes of violence. The 1982 California Commission on Crime Control and Violence Prevention report states clearly that, "Most current approaches to violence address its symptoms. Implicit in these approaches is the notion that our violence problems cannot be confronted, that X amount of violence is inevitable." But the report also gives a hopeful prognosis for the future: "There is nothing inevitable about the level of violence we currently experience. The United States ranks most violent among Western, industrialized democracies, not because persons living here are born more violent than those residing in Germany or Canada, but *because certain aspects of our social and cultural conditioning encourage violence*" [Emphasis added].

The report continues that this fact holds realistic hope for a less violent future because, once identified, those negative conditions can be remedied. It seems clear, and the report bears this out, that this malevolent social conditioning is directly related to what is happening in the family.

So far we have addressed only physical violence. There is, however, another manifestation of violence which is more subtle and which may actually be the conditioning for physically violent behavior in our society. This subtle form of violence is what noted psychiatrist Karl Meninger calls "selfism . . . the pseudo religion of ego-inflation and self-worship." He refers to a mentality which says, "Nobody's going to do that to me." This attitude, Meninger states, typifies a "primitive payback virus in people that gets us in a lot of trouble."

Such vengeful thinking is pervasive, reaching from the ghetto street gangs to the wealthiest aristocrat. In our society, where the well-to-do can acquire numerous possessions, the payback virus is complicated by the protectionist virus—where in addition to the "nobody's going to do that to me" mentality, there also exists the "nobody's going to take it away from me" mind frame.

This attitude motivates physical violence in the street and domestic violence and divorce in the home, because with this sort of thinking we put ourselves first. Putting ourselves before another person, even in our mind, does violence to that person. Putting ourselves before our marriage partners does violence to our marriage. It is hard to imagine how anyone with such a selfish attitude can ever hope for their marriage to endure. There may seem to be romance and sharing during the courting days and during the honeymoon, but when the crunch comes, the "me first" attitude will surface.

Nothing epitomizes the violence in our country, or the world, so much as the nuclear arms race. On New Year's Day 1978, Pope Paul VI said that violence in the world can be traced to the arms race and he called upon young people to reject violence even though war threatens them and the rest of humankind with "its supreme irrationality and its absurdity." He added that, "Such conditions of life provoke, especially among the young, frustrations which set off reactions of violence and aggressiveness against certain structures and economic situations of contemporary society."

No wonder the second most prevalent fear that children hold is the fear of nuclear war. Studies of the attitudes of children and youth regarding nuclear war were systematically begun in 1978 but not until recently have the results became widely known. One poll asked young people two questions: (1) Do you believe there will be a nuclear war, and (2) If so, do you believe you will survive it?

Even the pollsters were surprised when 84 percent of the youth answered "yes" to the first and "no" to the second. Harvey Cox, the Harvard Divinity School theologian, cited this statistic and said he was so skeptical he tried the same questions on one of his classes and was astounded when he obtained the same results. He commented, "These are not people who are living today as though there will be no tomorrow. We like to think of Harvard . . . as a place where people work now with the thought that in some future moment they will be able to give leadership in the various sectors of society. . . . These were young people who were staying up late nights working on projects and term papers and yet, in some dark region of their hearts, they don't believe there's any future that they are really preparing for."

College age youth are not the only ones plagued with these bleak thoughts. At a junior high school in our area a seventh grade boy wrote an article for the school paper which illustrates his thoughts of the future. It is so revealing, we are including the entire article here:

> The air was brown with dust from the unsettled ground. The ground was restless from each time a nuclear missile hit the soft soil. The radiation and the heat were overwhelming. That was two days ago. This is now.
>
> Jim and Terry climbed out of the lead-lined bunker. They were wearing gas masks and anti-radiation suits. Jim was wearing a .357 magnum pistol on his belt and their son, Keith, age 7, was sleeping.
>
> The war had started quite suddenly with a disagreement, and the first shot was fired. PEOPLE magazine had done a story on what might happen in

the event of nuclear war—now it was happening. Jim walked into the bunk-room and looked at his sleeping son and his dog Fonzie. There were three empty cots: one for him, one for his wife, and one for his other son, who was dead. He was killed after the first missile attack. He was in school when POW, missile #1 hit the center of the city. Jim had heard it on his radio. Faster than lightning he grabbed his son and wife and shot into the bunker. They had been there ever since. During that time they heard mutilated, but living, people trying to get in. His wife wanted to let at least one person in, but he refused, thinking that the person would either spread radiation all over the bunker or some kind of disease.

He thought about his dead son. Why did he have to leave me? Why couldn't he be sick like his little brother? We miss you so much. Goodbye, my son.

He walked out into the bunker storage area where he checked the food supply. Enough, he thought, to last a while. By the time they ran out, he could go hunting for whatever lived. He had enough rifles and ammo to last a couple years. He hoped they would last that long.

Surely if parents knew what went on in their children's minds they would be shocked. Such a story is full of psychological clues even lay people like ourselves can recognize. What is most revealing, however, is this boy's thoughts of violence and "selfism" which accompany his thoughts regarding nuclear war. They all form part of the big picture.

Nuclear fears may differ somewhat with sex and economic class but you can be certain they are there. Our first awareness of this was when our youngest son, Mark, was about nine. We were looking at a publication which had a mushroom cloud on the cover. Mark hesitantly asked if a nuclear bomb hit right on a bomb shelter, would it blow the shelter up. Taken aback we replied yes, a direct hit would destroy the shelter. He responded almost vehemently: "Then what good are they?" While searching for an answer we looked into Mark's eyes. The fear was unmasked. "Do you think about this quite a bit, Mark?" we asked. He looked a little shy but nodded affirmatively. Up until that time we had discussed nuclear war and antinuclear actions around our house without too much thought to what the younger ones were absorbing. We then realized the necessity of prudence about what conversations the children are allowed to overhear.

This doesn't imply that we should keep our children in a vacuum. That would not work anyway for they are too smart. What they do not learn at home they will get from their peers, possibly in a distorted fashion. What we do mean is that we should present the problem to them in proper context, with an ample measure of hope and a good understanding of our power to offset every grisly aspect. As with everything else in child rearing, our best contribution is our example. Seeing us do things to stop this menace will give them more of a sense of security than all the words we can formulate.

One father, Bill Drake, wrote an essay to help parents and teachers deal with children's nuclear fears. His general approach is divided into three stages according to age. During the first seven years, or "until the age of teeth," play is the most important learning activity. They live in a world of imagination and fantasy. Much of the children's behavior is spent acting out examples they have seen. Our responsibility as parents is to provide wholesome examples along with happiness and security. Positive and negative patterns are developed in these years so emphasis should be on the positive. As much as possible, the child should be spared concern about nuclear war.

The next seven years, about seven to 14, is a time when feelings are developed. This is the time to present beautiful and hopeful vistas. During the first part of this time children begin to discriminate or, as Bill describes it, they tend to transform from holistic to dualistic perception and begin to feel a distinction between themselves and their surroundings. Self-consciousness increases and parents have to use particular tact and patience to give the children the careful guidance they want and need. Later in this age bracket, children begin to comprehend time sequence. They acquire some perception of history and at this juncture parents should emphasize peacemaking and discuss with their children how unwise and unthinking activity can get out of hand—what would happen if everyone does it. Governments, and responsible behavior of governments, can also be touched upon. If the children ask questions about nuclear war, they should be given honest answers but not saturated with morbid details.

It is during the third seven-year period—roughly 14 to 21, varying according to individual development—that the intellect slowly develops. During the early part of this age it is well to discuss the responsibilities that go with freedom. Later we can acknowledge the mess the world is in, in a community sense—that is, the problem we are challenged with—and explore ways to improve conditions. Nuclear war questions can be handled in more frank detail and guiding information can be volunteered. Older teenagers can really start getting involved with alternatives. Again, however, it is the manner in which we parents help our youth to understand the problems which will set the scene for anything from utter hopelessness to a firm determination to assert personal power.

This is the general approach Bill outlines which is really nothing more than parental common sense and the means we would use to teach our children about other "worldly" matters. The important thing to remember is not to introduce fears the child does not have and to deal constructively with the fears that are there.

Children's war fears have become so worrisome that the U.S. House of Representatives' Select Committee on Children, Youth and Families held hearings during September 1983. Three children—two girls and a boy, ages eleven to 16—testified along with one of the children's fathers. Three psychiatrists and a pediatrician also testified. Ursell Austin, 16, told the committee:

> I think about the bomb just about every day now. It makes me sad and depressed when I think about a bomb ever being dropped. I hope I'm with my family. I don't want to die alone. I think about it most on sunny days when I'm having a good time. I think—it could happen right now.

I thought about it when I was going to camp, because I kept thinking, what if a nuclear war happens when I'm away from home and away from my family. I was afraid of coming back from camp and there would be nothing left.

One of the things I think about is what it would be like when a warning comes. I would try to get my family together, go to my grandma's house where we could hold each other tight and pray. I don't want to be warned. I don't want to know it is about to happen. If it is going to happen, I want to be killed right away. Being alive during or after the bomb would be the most frightening of all. I think surviving would be worse than dying.

At the time of her testimony, Ursell was in the age bracket when the intellect is nearing maturation. It is a time when parents and teachers should be working creatively to help children realize their potential. Unfortunately, we are faced with the nuclear picture and it will not go away by just ignoring it.

Robert Fiedler, father of one of the children testifying, told the committee that "they're afraid they're not going to grow up. What do you say when youngsters say, as they have to me, 'If I get married I'm not going to have kids because I don't want them to die in a nuclear war.' You can't throw them a lie. Before the nuclear age we had the luxury of being ignorant of the devastation wars caused. We were able to limit the degree of civilization we would destroy. Today we're not talking about World War II or World War I—the kids understand."

Yes, the children certainly do understand. Robert's eleven-year-old daughter, Jessica, told the congressional committee, "Some people say you can live through a nuclear war. Maybe a few people would, but when they run out of food, they can't go to the local supermarket, it won't be there."

Fear of nuclear war is reaching down to younger and younger children. During the hearings, psychiatrist John E. Mack explained, "Children as young as five or six are expressing fears to their parents and teachers about nuclear destruction and not growing up. Young children, ages six to nine, seem particularly afraid that they will be abandoned and left alone in a nuclear war; that is, that they will survive while their family and friends are killed. . . . Some children voice curiosity about what it is like to experience different age periods, as they do not expect to reach them themselves."

In his concluding testimony, Dr. Robert Jay Lifton described the "double life" which children live: "On the one hand they go about their everyday activities—their studies and exams at school, their pleasure and struggles in their families, their preparation for adult life. But on the other hand, they express the fearful sense that all of this is a sham, that they are preparing for nothingness, that there will be no adult existence. The double life exists for the rest of us as well; we know that our world is such that at any given moment everything and everyone we have touched or loved could be annihilated, yet we go about business as usual as though no such danger exists."

People often become desperate when they are faced with what seems to be a hopelessly overpowering situation. For decades it has been recognized that poverty leads to reckless crimes and other social disorders. That recklessness is being further aggravated today by the nuclear shadow. The nuclear threat is now accepted as a major contributor to social problems such as drugs, alcohol, crime, immorality and suicide. Addressing only the latter, suicide ranks second only to accidents as the leading killer among youth. Death rates are declining in every age bracket except for those under 25. Furthermore, suicide may be more of a killer than actually reported because many accidents and drug overdoses could be intentional, and many suicides are covered up to prevent family embarrassment. Nevertheless, counting only the reported suicides, since the mid-1960s the suicide rate has tripled among youth from 15 to 24 years old.

Fear in the family is a formidable force to confront but confront it we must if we are to raise mentally healthy children with wholesome outlooks; children who will contribute significantly to the transformation of society. In the case of nuclear fear, we parents face a real challenge. The main source of hope for the children is our involvement in the solution. Action brings hope to us as well as to our children. They feel more secure when they see us working for their safety. As Dr. Lifton pointed out: "Our choice then is not whether we wish our children to know or not to know about the nuclear threat, but rather whether we can have the wisdom and responsibility to share knowledge with them and bring them into our counsels. If done properly, with specific sensitivity to age groups and individuals, and by combining the message of danger with assertions of human possibilities, such teaching is the very opposite of the 'death trip.' It is indeed an expression of hope."

We are trying to put these ideas to work in our family. Since we are involved in the antinuclear movement, we have discussions and meetings in our home, yet we have learned to temper the talk so as not to overwhelm youngsters who may be within earshot. We discuss events such as television programs with them, and we emphasize the fact that we are not alone—that through our community effort we will overcome the nuclear threat. The feeling of working together with others has given hope.

The other night we were watching a television show depicting what children in Russia think about nuclear war. Mark seemed to be impressed that the children there answered questions about the same as he would, but the greatest bonding seemed to occur when the Soviet children were asked if they thought bomb shelters and civil defense would protect them. One girl started her answer with an emphatic "Nyet!" Mark didn't have to wait for the translation. He became animated and repeated "Nyet!" We could see he thought these were just plain kids who think the same as he did and knew the same answers. Mark could sense some unity with these faraway Soviet children through not only sharing their feelings, but also understanding their language— although it was only one word.

Sometimes when Mark looks worried we just make a spirited exclamation like, "Mark, we're going to whip this thing. We're making headway and with God's help we're going to do it." That usually brings a guarded grin. The happy part is that we believe every word of it. We think that down deep Mark does also.

Afterword

I may have all knowledge
    and understand all secrets;
I may have all the faith
   needed to move mountains;
But if I have not love,
  I am nothing.
I may give away everything
    I have,
And even give up my body
    to be burned;
But if I have not love;
    it does me no good.
       —1 Corinthians 13: 2-3

For many years we have wondered if there would be any advantage in relating our experiences, successes and failures to others and have attempted this to a limited extent in some magazine articles. In late summer of 1979 we were invited to Japan to participate in a conference and then go on a speaking tour. While flying at 40,000 feet above the Pacific the idea germinated to write a book together. We drew up the chapter outlines in a Tokyo hotel room. Upon our return home we started writing. After many long years this is the result.

We did not write this book because we have been successful in all the aspects of marriage and family life mentioned. A good share of our knowledge comes from mistakes and failures. For that reason, this is not a "how to" book on raising children to be nonviolent. It is merely a collection of our experiences and thoughts which we wish to share in the hope they will help other parents become more aware earlier in their children's lives.

It has probably already become obvious that love is the real name for nonviolence. When we chose the title for this book, we really meant parenting with love. Nonviolence (love) is the stuff and substance of a wholesome family. It is the key to successful parenting. No one holds a franchise on it. It is there for every husband, wife, mother, father and child—it is available to everyone.

Love is the binding thread which weaves through the chapters of this book to hold all of our experiences together; just as it weaves through our family to hold all of us together. Love is our real message.

Love is what has saved us from being miserable flops as parents and marriage partners. It covers up many human weaknesses. It is the energy that remains in memory when less pleasant events are long forgotten. Love is the real energy in marriage and family.

So our book on nonviolence in the family is really about love. It is also about the family as a community of love. We have always emphasized the family as the core community. Ideally, it is a community within a community of families which are helping to support each other. That ideal is becoming harder to achieve in today's unthinking, uncaring mass society. The positive side, however, is that our ability to reason and care is evolving at least as fast as the birth rate and with a little more application of these abilities that ideal can be approached.

The other night Bob had a dream that all the back yard fences in our block fell down. (Actually, that part of the dream was close to happening.) The nice part about that dream was that all the families decided not to build them up again. Instead, we made a park out of our block and it was a beautiful place to live. The children had space to run and play. At one end we planted a community garden. We pooled our tools, equipment, lawn furniture, jungle gyms and labor to make life simpler and more pleasant while at the same time reducing consumption— which is a plague on poor countries.

Maybe some day that dream will come true.

During a recent discussion with one of our friends, we mentioned that the family, living up to its ideal, is the key to society's problems. Our friend quickly disagreed, feeling that whatever the remedial structure would be, surely returning to past family structures was not the answer. Our disagreement seemed to stem from a misconception that we meant restoring the family to some structure it had in the past. So we rephrased our statement, pointing out that the problems in society result from the failure of the family to accomplish its function—to which our friend agreed. Then we suggested that if we could correct what is breaking down in the family we could alleviate most of today's problems. Again there was agreement. So then we pointed out that this community of family communities is what we visualize as the structure of a society which would bring peace and justice, joy and harmony. Such a relationship would not be a recreating of the past because it is something that has never been fully achieved. It could very well be this new structure which our friend envisions but cannot formulate.

So when we say the family community is the hope of society, we are not referring to antiquated structures. We perceive deeper family ties when love is not only present but visibly demonstrated. This is the family community which will transform society—the constituent in the community of communities which will become our future society.

Transformation will not happen if we just sit back. It will take sweat, determination, perseverance, commitment and vision. Although not an easy accomplishment, we believe this transformed society will someday come into being. How soon that will happen depends on us. Some families are approaching that goal now and it is their influence which keeps our society from becoming completely chaotic. As more of us move toward perfecting our families as communities of love, we will see formidable changes taking place in the wider community of society.

We all have slightly different ideas. We all have fragile egos and other human weaknesses. Also, we have the capacity to love and be loved. Love should be our primary focus because it has the power to achieve many things.

Additional copies available from your local bookstore or by sending $9.45 for each copy, postpaid, to:

Hope Publishing House
P.O. Box 60008
Pasadena, CA 91106